PERSONAL FINANCE For TEENS

REAL WORLD MONEY MANAGEMENT EXERCISES: BUILD FINANCIAL LITERACY SKILLS, START ADULTING WITH YOUR MONEY, AND CONTROL YOUR FUTURE TODAY!

WILLIAM P. BURKE

CONTENTS

Introduction 1

Chapter 1: **Your Literacy Rate** 5

    What Is Financial Literacy?   6

    Back on the Daily Grind   7

    What They Don't Teach You   9

    Financial Management   9

    Essential Financial Lessons for Teens   11

    The Real World . . .   14

    Summary   15

    Exercise   17

    Endnotes   19

Chapter 2: **The One About Saving** 21

    Love and Other Drugs   22

    Necessary Evils   23

    You Have to Decide   24

    Steps to Saving   25

    Smarties   28

    The Real World . . .   29

    Summary   30

    Exercise   33

    Endnotes   35

Chapter 3: **Ballin' on a Budget** 37

    Basics   38

    Picking Your Strategy   40

    The Game Plan   41

Hit the App Store   44

The Real World . . .   45

Summary   46

Exercise   48

Endnotes   49

Chapter 4: **Stash Your Cash** **51**

First Things First . . .   52

Benefits on Benefits   53

Teens + Jobs = $$$ 53

Banking Basics   57

Deep Pockets, De-Posits   57

Counting Your Accounts   58

Card Shark   59

Bank Statements   60

You Try It Now   61

Before You Retire . . .   63

The Real World . . .   64

Summary   66

Exercise   68

Endnotes   69

Chapter 5: **You Really Are Just a Number, AKA, The One About Credit** **71**

The Ghosts of Credit's Past, Present, and Future   72

Understanding Your Credit   73

Why Do I Care?   75

How to Start   76

Loans and Tigers and Bears, Oh My   77

Interesting   77

Again, Why Do I Care?   80

The Real World . . .   81

Summary   82

Exercise   84

Endnotes   86

Chapter 6: **Wait, I Can Invest??** **89**

The Wolf of Main Street   90

Chart the Course   91

Brokerage > Going Broke   93

Start It Up   95

Other Options   96

The Real World . . .   97

Summary   98

Exercise   101

Endnotes   102

Chapter 7: **Shut Up and Take My Money** **103**

Bonds. Stocks and Bonds.   104

Mutual Funds   106

Exchange-Traded Funds   106

Certificates of Deposit (CDs)   107

Retirement Plans   107

Options   108

Annuities   108

Commodities   109

Real Estate and Property Investments   109

How to Get Started   114

Entrepreneurship and Business   117

The Real World . . .   121

Summary   122

Exercise   124

Endnotes   126

Chapter 8: **The Tax Talk** **129**

    Taxation Without Representation   129

    The Real World . . .   134

    Summary   136

    Exercise   138

    Endnotes   139

Chapter 9: **Send Scammers to the Junk Folder** **141**

    Techy Teens   142

    Common Scams   143

    Fighting Back   147

    Fraud Prevention   148

    The Real World . . .   151

    Summary   153

    Exercise   155

    Endnotes   157

Chapter 10: **College . . . Is It for Me? How to Save and Prepare**   **159**

    Is College Right for You?   160

    What Are Student Loans?   161

    Tips on Saving for College - A Teen's Guide   164

    Getting Your Teens Involved in Saving   166

    Having "That Talk" with Your Teen   167

    The Real World . . .   169

    Summary   170

    Exercise   172

    Endnotes   174

Conclusion **177**

INTRODUCTION

*M*y sincere hope is that you never walk through my doors and ask for my services.

Sounds counterproductive, right? After all, my job *is* offering financial advice. I've spent 20 years of my life correcting and advising folks on their financial decisions.

The more people that walk into my offices, the more money in my pocket. That means more food on my table, more memorable family vacations, and more choices when it comes to my kids' educational future.

But seriously, this book will have done its job if you never need me.

I don't mean that in some "holier than thou" way. My work is a bit like a lawyer's—when people come to my office, it's generally because something has gone wrong. They have significant debt and need restructuring. They're behind on loan payments and need help charting a path forward.

What I've learned after over 20 years in the world of finance is that many of the problems afflicting my clients stem from one source. Failing to understand the fundamentals of credit, an inability to make a budget, or a repulsion to saving are merely symptoms of a singular problem: a startling lack of education related to personal finance.

The best way that I've found to curb this drought is by starting young. As a father of five, I've worked closely with my own kids to develop strong financial habits that will pay dividends down the road.

In addition, it's no secret that some of the most financially insecure sections of our population are teens. That's not my own diagnosis; it's one supported by numerous studies. A whopping 75% of teens lack confidence in their knowledge of personal finance.[1]

When it comes to the specifics of personal finance, we see the same patterns. For instance, despite 86% of teens expressing an interest in investing, fewer than 50% actually did so in 2023, citing a lack of confidence as the key reason. 41% of teens are unfamiliar with a 401(k), and 32% couldn't tell you the difference between a credit card and a debit card.[2]

The educational deficit isn't just limited to retirement accounts; teens report a lack of instruction regarding simple concepts like saving (62%), earning (50%), saving for college (44%), and budgeting (42%).[3]

The easy explanation is a lack of interest from teens, who are too busy filming the latest dance craze on TikTok or buying clothes from influencers on Instagram.

But that notion vastly underestimates teens' interest in personal finance. Almost the same number of teens who have a lack of confidence surrounding personal finance (75%) also *want* more personal finance education (73%).

As the stats show, teens aren't alone in their desire to take control of their financial future. But beginning the journey toward a better financial future can be scary. With adults constantly throwing "advice" their way, it can feel overwhelming even to start. This leads to burnout and, more often than not, to a seat in my office.

Consider this book one of the first steps along the road of a lifetime of financial freedom. Even better, it's a tool to separate the information you actually need from the noise. In it, we'll offer shortcuts that your parents wish they knew when they started.

For example, instead of telling you to set aside money, we'll offer three proven methods of budgeting. Rather than tell you to invest, we'll walk through how, even as a teen, you can put your hard-earned money to work and how to go about selecting the right types of investment. And rather than tell you to prepare for college, you'll get a crash course on how to know if college is right for you and actual steps you can take to keep your loans at a minimum. And that's just the start!

In short, this book is going to cut through the nonsense and weed out the erroneous advice that often comes from venturing down the personal finance rabbit hole on YouTube or Google.

And this book is about more than merely learning how to put money in your pocket. It's about a lifetime of happiness and stability. Starting as a teen and building strong habits is an instrumental part of finding your future happiness. As one financial influencer vividly described:

"Yes, technically happiness is not something you can go out and buy. And there is a point at which more money will mean diminishing returns in the terms of day-to-day fulfillment. But money buys stability, relaxation, the ability to focus on what you want, free time, and help with various life tasks. It means that an unexpected expense won't spiral into a dismantled life. It means peace of mind about the future. It means options."[4]

By the end, you'll have a solid foundation to begin a life of personal finance freedom, which means more time scrolling on Twitter and less time scrounging for pennies.

Let me paint the picture of life without this book.

Say you're one of the 32% of teens who don't know the difference between a credit card and a debit card. You rack up charge after charge on your credit card until it crashes hard on its $3,000 limit. At your part-time job, you earn $150 per week or around $600 per month. For starters, it would take five months to ultimately pay off your credit card.

By then, you've likely missed several payments, sending your credit score spiraling. You probably also have several mandatory monthly expenses, including a cell phone bill, Spotify subscription, or car insurance, meaning you're adding more charges as you pay off the old ones.

That money only disappears by paying it off. And until you do, that money will hang around like the zit that just won't go away. It will control *you* instead of vice versa.

As a teen, if your future brings you more anxiety than a pre-calculus test, you aren't alone. In fact, you're in just the right place. It's time to take control of your money.

Let's get started.

ENDNOTES

1. Turner, T. (2023, August 11). 47+ Fascinating Financial Literacy Statistics in 2023, *Annuity*. https://www.annuity.org/financial-literacy/financial-literacy-statistics/.

2. Ibid.

3. Ibid.

4. The Financial Diet. (2021, May 21). *Sunday reminder: money may not buy happiness, but it definitely provides stability* [Link attached] [Post]. Instagram. https://www.instagram.com/p/Csgw1lTOKxi/?igshid=MzRlODBiNWFlZA==.

Chapter 1

YOUR LITERACY RATE

It's not how much money you make, but how much money you keep, how hard it works for you and how many generations you keep it for.
   —Robert Kiyosaki

Money is numbers and numbers never end. If it takes money to be happy, your search for happiness will never end.
   —Bob Marley

Plastered on a wall somewhere, probably in your school, is a sign that reads "a journey of a thousand miles begins with a single step." Perhaps there are footprints trudging along a sandy beach. Or a bridge connecting two dangerous mountain peaks. A road that disappears into a foggy unknown.

That's cool and all. But what happens when your car runs out of fuel? Or you slice open your foot on a jagged seashell? Or, god forbid, that rotted out bridge crumples as soon as you take that first step?

You'll need gas. Or insurance. Or a good lawyer.

Either way, it's going to cost money. So sure, you can start your journey with a single step, but you'll probably need more than a few singles in the bank account to get you where you want to go.

In other words, you'll need to be financially literate.

WHAT IS FINANCIAL LITERACY?

The world of finance is full of complicated lingo, contradictory rules, and run by people who brag about their "Home in the Hamptons."

At least, that's what most people assume. The truth is, finance is accessible to just about anyone willing to put in the time and energy to become **financially literate**. Financial literacy is the ability to understand and effectively use various financial skills, including personal financial management, budgeting, and investing.[1]

In other words, financial literacy is your ticket to organizing all of that confusing information.

Think about financial literacy like Instagram. On the surface, everything seems simple: snap a picture and post it.

But is Instagram really just about sharing photos? As aspiring influencers will tell you—no! There are dozens of features—applying filters, sponsored ads, Instagram Reels, sponsored ads, Instagram storefronts, and DMs, just to name a few. Understanding how these features work allows you to take full advantage of the app and avoid public humiliation from your friends.

Similarly, financial literacy, when boiled down to its most basic concept, is about saving and spending money. But under the surface are a handful of additional concepts: earning, investing, borrowing and managing debt, planning, and protecting your assets.[2]

And while high school humiliation definitely feels like the end of the world in the moment, the consequences of being financially illiterate are potentially much worse. For instance, you can always transfer high schools when your ex-best friend posts an earth-shatteringly embarrassing pic on Instagram. But you can only outrun credit card debt for so long.

Not buying it? Think about the consequences of defaulting on that debt: your ability to buy a house, a car, or land a loan to start the business of your dreams is all tied to that decision. Financial literacy helps you avoid those dangers and keeps your financial future secure.

The scope of financial literacy generally covers the following areas:

- Household budgeting
- Debt management (i.e. cell phone loan, car loans, student loans, mortgages, bank loans, health insurance)
- Credit card evaluation and selection
- Short and long-term financial planning
- Investment vehicles

Don't worry so much about what each of those means right now. Just know this: financial literacy concerns just about every aspect of your money.

And because we're talking about your money, the benefits to being financially literate are massive. It's the difference between preventing devastating mistakes and being swallowed by debt. Or preparing for emergencies and choosing between a new car transmission or groceries. Or reaching your financial goals early or working until you're 80.

But perhaps the most important benefit is the confidence factor. Many people make poor financial decisions because they aren't confident in the decision that they're making. This stems directly from a lack of financial literacy. It's like showing up for an algebra test having missed the entire chapter on linear equations. How confident would you be about acing that exam?

On the other hand, financial literacy allows you to lead with confidence and take control of your financial future.

BACK ON THE DAILY GRIND

There's no magic wand to becoming financially literate. The only way to a financially literate future is by putting in the work, which, admittedly, isn't always the most exciting thing in the world.

But is it as painful as boxing? Probably not. And yet, here's a bit of inspiration from legendary boxer and activist Muhammad Ali about putting in the work to reap the rewards:

> *"I hated every minute of training, but I said, don't quit, suffer now and live the rest of your life as a champion."*

You may never be in a championship prizefight, a World Cup pitch, or take the last shot in Game Five of the WNBA Finals. But personal finance is a personal championship for yourself. Every moment that you train puts you one step closer to controlling your money without letting your money control you.

Which brings us to the f-word. For some teens, it's scary. For others, it's not something worth thinking about. Heck, you didn't even study linear equations for your test tomorrow. Why should you be concerned about something that's years away?

Because the "future" is coming quicker than you think. Home ownership, car loans, and a retirement account might actually be a ways off (although it doesn't have to be), but others are right on the horizon.

Think about student loans. Is it borderline criminal that your 18-year-old self shackles your ankles to thousands of dollars of student debt that your 28-year-old self is still dealing with? Probably. But understanding personal finances as a teen can help mitigate that issue.

Or credit cards. Several high-profile banks have *no age minimum* when it comes to opening a credit card account.[3] Others set minimum ages between 13-18 years old. 1 in 6 teens has a credit card (and 46% of parents have caught their kids using their credit cards).[4]

The point is, financial tools are *everywhere*. And they're being used by teens (whether they're supposed to or not).

And chances are, unless you take it upon yourself to learn about personal finance, you aren't getting any lessons elsewhere. In the American classroom, students are taught about saving money as early as fifth grade and . . . then it just sort of stops.[5]

WHAT THEY DON'T TEACH YOU

It doesn't make much sense, that some of the most practical life advice isn't being taught in schools. And outside of schools, where else are you supposed to learn this stuff? CNBC? Fox Business? A newspaper?!

Some folks might be lucky enough to get some training from a financially-savvy parent. But those parents were also confused teens once. And many of them are *still* those confused teens, hardly in a place to offer financial advice. As one writer put it:

> *For parents—the topic of money is almost like sex—they never want to talk about it with their children. They may be uneducated themselves, or they may not want their kids knowing how much they make.*[6]

The simple truth is, the earlier you start building good financial habits, the better. That's obvious. You don't have to be Merrill or Lynch for that to make sense.

FINANCIAL MANAGEMENT

If you're one of the 86% of teens out there, then you want to start investing.[7] But every time you click the Stocks app on your iPhone, some guy named Dow Jones shows up along with what looks like his heart monitor? And, you're no doctor, but Mr. Jones' heart rate is a bit all over the place.

Step one: exit the Stocks app. Pronto. The big stock market lesson is coming, but the first step to investing (and making any good financial decision) doesn't involve Dow Jones or QQQ (whatever that is).

The very first thing to do is develop a healthy relationship with money. Remember: humans have been around long before money came around. Humans invented money. Humans assign money its worth, figuratively and literally.

And yet, humans' relationship with money is often the other way around. Individuals become controlled by it. It consumes every waking moment of their day. They break the law in its name. That, much like Barbie and Ken, Oppenheimer and Jean Tatlock, or Oppenheimer and the atomic bomb, is an unhealthy relationship.

Here are a handful of tips to build a healthy relationship with money:

- **Discuss money matters with your family**
  You need someone to feel comfortable talking to, and family is forever. Like taking out the trash and brushing your teeth, building healthy financial habits starts at home.

- **Practice transparency**
  Think of being secretive about your money as the opening act in a life of bad money habits. It's the tip of the iceberg. The first skid on the slipperiest slope. Being honest and open allows you to make the best financial decision. It also let's those who you trust to give the most complete advice.

- **Don't feel guilty for spending**
  The conventional problem is people spending more money than they have. But at the other end of the spectrum sits militant saving. This also creates an unhealthy relationship with money because you're still allowing the money to control you and your decisions rather than vice versa.

- **Don't compare your finances to that of your friends**
  Comparison is the root of so many unhealthy habits: you can either become jealous of what someone else has, or, on the contrary, put others down for not having as much as you. Remember that we're all in the same ocean, floating in different boats, but generally rowing in the same direction. Your friends' ability to buy a car sooner than you says nothing about who you are as a person, your character, or, frankly, even anything about them.

At the end of the day, you are not your money. Traits like kindness, honesty, and empathy should make up your purpose. Those characteristics should form your north star. If money is guiding your life, you're in an unhealthy relationship.

ESSENTIAL FINANCIAL LESSONS FOR TEENS

With the foundations of a good relationship in place, it's time to start talking practically about how finances work. According to the finance site Medi-Share, there are 10 essential ideas every teen should grasp in order to properly manage their money.[8] These will be tackled in greater detail in the coming chapters, but here's a quick primer:

1. **Needs vs Wants.** An important first step in making smart financial decisions is separating needs from wants. And be honest with yourself here: you may need a pair of cleats for soccer, but want the recently dropped magenta Nike Mercurials.

2. **Spend Less Than You Earn, Save the Difference.** As a teenager, your expenses are going to be pretty low. You might want some money to spend hanging with friends, but you probably don't have a car payment, rent, or utilities to pay off every month. As a result, your teens are one of the best chances to save the difference between what you earn and what you spend.

3. **Track Expenses and Start a Budget.** But in order to figure out how much you can save every month, you need to have a budget. And in order to have a budget, you need to figure out how much you have in expenses every month. Once you have an idea of how much money goes out, you'll know how much money you need to bring in and how much money you get to keep after paying those expenses.

4. **Save, but Start Investing Early.** Saving is only part of the game. Investing is a great way to have your money work for you. By putting some money away in a retirement account or mutual fund (don't worry, we'll get there), you'll start to see whatever you put in expand in value and size.

5. **Use the Power of Compound Interest.** How does it "expand in value and size," you ask? Through something called compound interest. You might have heard about loans accruing interest, meaning a borrower is forced to pay more money than what they initially took out. But this works the other way too; you're able to *earn* interest on money you deposit, meaning your money can grow with only a single deposit.

6. **Understand Gross versus Net Pay.** Regardless of your job type, you'll probably be given some version of a monthly salary. That's what's known as "gross pay"—it's the amount of money a job pays before tax and insurance withholdings. Once the money is taken out, your paycheck reflects "net pay." In the short-term it's a bummer. But long-term it'll save you the headache of organizing taxes in March.

7. **Good versus Bad Debt.** Is there such a thing as "good" debt? Believe it or not—yes! Good debt is any debt that helps you reach your goals and has manageable interest rates. For instance, student loans might be considered a form of good debt—after all, they help the borrower achieve their goals of getting an education.

    But those same loans could be considered bad debt. While many student loans are backed up by the Department of Education, others are purely to get your money, and lots of it for that matter. They carry extremely high interest rates (meaning you'll end up paying back *way* more than you borrow) and are designed to *take advantage* of a borrower instead of help them (this is called 'predatory lending').

8. **Your Credit Score Matters.** What if there was a magical number that essentially determined if you could own your own home, your own car, or take out a business loan? For better or worse, there is: your credit score. In short, your credit score is a way to assess how likely you are to pay back your debts. Building up good credit in your teens could help your long-term credit goals, while being lax about paying off your cards on time as a teen could seriously hurt your credit goals.

9. **Big Loans Can Really Affect Your Life.** Before taking out tons of loans, it's important to be realistic about your future. That includes getting into the weeds about what job you want to have, starting salaries, and probable future expenses. Loans are helpful, but they can also cause a lot of agony—late nights trying to balance your accounts, working overtime to make payments, etc. Think long and hard about your future before making promises to pay back tons of borrowed cash.

10. **You Can Be an Entrepreneur Without Taking on Much Debt.** One way of going about starting a brand new business is by taking out a loan to fund the things necessary to pull it off. Say, for instance, you start a podcast. You *could* take out loans to purchase microphones, headsets, camera equipment, and a sound mixer. But what happens if you decide podcasting isn't for you? Suddenly you're stuck with debt and boxes of equipment. Instead, you can find ways to start out cheaply and put whatever money you have into marketing your business and developing a network of fans. Then, any money you make from the podcast goes directly back into the business, instead of paying off those loans, meaning quicker growth!

THE REAL WORLD . . . In a moment, you'll be asked to think about what you want your future to look like. That includes whether you want to go to college, what type of job you think you might want, and how to use finances to get you across the finish line.

But it's also helpful to think about the advice your future self would give you. First, study for that algebra test. That's a given.

While the specifics are impossible to think about (not to get too meta, but your future self can't give you advice about *that* relationship because your present self doesn't know about it yet), it is possible to think a little more abstractly.

That's exactly what 27-year-old journalist Zina Kumok did when she wrote a short note to her 17-year-old self. *"Save more money, spend less on eating out and shopping, and apply for every scholarship possible."* [9]

Kumok's letter strikes at the heart of being financially literate as a teenager. Saving money? Spending less? Finding creative ways to get an education and start a business? This is financial literacy in action!

SUMMARY

Here are the Top Five Mistakes Teens Make When it Comes to Financial Literacy

1. Starting Too Late
The earlier you start, the better. That lesson applies to just about everything—studying for a math test, learning to drive a car—but is especially true for financial literacy. By starting now, you'll begin developing the skills and good habits necessary to thrive when it matters most.

2. Taking Out Too Much Debt Early
Whether it's student loan debt or taking out a loan for a new car, it's easy to be sucked into borrowing money for wants instead of needs. Be proactive about budgeting and your professional future by developing creative ways to earn money that don't include monthly payment plans.

**3. Developing Bad Habits and
   a Bad Relationship With Money**
It's easy to feel like a handful of dead presidents control your life when you're in a toxic relationship with money. Becoming financially literate will help you take the reigns back on your future and your money, ensuring that you're in charge, not a piece of paper or plastic.

4. Feeling Alone
Some folks are private about their money, making the road to personal finance feel cold and lonely. But never forget that you aren't alone; your parents likely struggled with the same difficult finance decisions, as did their parents. Don't be afraid to ask questions. After all, you don't want your money to control you!

5. Giving Up

Personal finance requires significant perseverance. It won't always be easy. You won't always want to save money. It'll feel nauseating as you grind away at a budget (or maybe not!). But quitting is the *only* real way to fail at this once you get started. It's like the line we began the chapter with— your journey to financial literacy begins one step at a time. Always move forward, even on the hardest days.

Doing even a tiny bit of financial planning as a teenager can make hundreds of thousands of dollars of difference! But it takes intentionality; financial planning requires that you put in the work to learn the system so that you can make wise decisions for your future (ah! The f-word again!).

EXERCISE

The following are exercises designed to get you thinking about financial literacy and personal finance.

Develop a Budget.
Go back through your last month and tally up the total amount of your expenses. Then, add up all the money you earned, be it from chores, a job, or an allowance.

If you're making less than you spend, great work! Determine how much you could save each month based on that positive difference.

If you're spending more than you make, you have a bit of work to do. Figure out what of those expenses are "wants" versus "needs" and begin by trimming down the "want" purchases. Repeat these steps the following month and see how well you did at keeping to your budget!

BEGIN BY . . . While some budgeting services require a paid subscription, you can do this step for free with a pad of paper and a pen, or a Microsoft Excel spreadsheet.

Think About the Future
Much of this process involves being deliberate about what you want your future to look like. With that in mind, write out any specific goals you have for yourself. It could be as soon as acing a test next week, or as distant as retiring by age 50.

Then, consider how your personal finances can get you to those places. For instance, if you want to graduate college with a degree in finance, write down what steps can you start taking *now* to get there. That might mean researching loan options and college tuition costs, as

(continued) EXERCISE

well as determining a potential starting salary after you graduate.

Don't hold anything back—this is for your own personal use. Whatever dreams you may have, put pen to paper and start working out how to make them a reality.

BEGIN BY ... Imagine where you'd like your life to be in the next five, 10, or 15 years. Write down whatever dreams, hopes, or goals you'd like to accomplish.

Talk to Your Parents or Family

A lack of transparency and honesty about finances is how a bad relationship with money is formed. Get ahead of that by being proactive in having conversations with your parents. You might ask them how they budget, or what they do on a monthly basis to make sure expenses are paid.

Don't forget that your parents are also much older than you, and by extension, far more experienced. They'll likely have stories about their own finance situations that might be useful to learn from.

BEGIN BY ... Ask you parents one financial thing they're proud of doing and one thing they wish that they had done sooner.

ENDNOTES

1. Fernando, J. (2023, March 30). *Financial Literacy: What it is, and why it's so important.* Investopedia. https://www.investopedia.com/terms/f/financial-literacy.asp

2. Turner, T. (2023, August 14). *Financial Literary: The 5 Principles Explained.* Annuity. https://www.annuity.org/financial-literacy/

3. White, A. (2023, May 23). *What is the minimum age to be an authorized user on a credit card?* CNBC. https://www.cnbc.com/select/whats-the-minimum-age-to-be-an-authorized-user-on-a-credit-card/

4. Papandrea, D. (2022, March 1). *46% of Parents Say Their Child Used Their Credit or Debit Card Without Permission, Racking Up $500+.* LendingTree. https://www.lendingtree.com/credit-cards/study/kids-and-credit-cards-survey/

5. Minnium, A. (2013, June 9). Why Teens Need to Learn About Personal Finance. *Wall Street Journal.* https://www.wsj.com/articles/SB10001424127887323415304578368712024745432

6. Ibid.

7. Paulus, N. (2023, May 15). *Teens' Guide to Building a Strong Personal Finance Foundation.* MoneyGeek. https://www.moneygeek.com/financial-planning/personal-finance-for-teens/

8. Medi-Share. (2019, October 18). *10 Essential Financial Lessons for Teens.* https://www.medishare.com/blog/10-essential-money-lessons-every-teen-should-learn

9. Snider, S. (2016, September 8). *Dear Younger Me: 12 Financial Truths We Wish We Knew Earlier.* US News and World Report. https://money.usnews.com/money/personal-finance/slideshows/dear-younger-me-12-financial-truths-we-wish-we-knew-earlier?slide=2

Chapter 2

THE ONE ABOUT SAVING

A simple fact that is hard to learn is that the time to save money is when you have some.
—Joe Moore

A wise person should have money in their head, not in their heart.
—Jonathan Swift

Isn't the point of having money to make life easier? Didn't a bunch of people invent money because exchanging cows for car washes was getting out of hand? And because the exchange rate between a French hen and a Portuguese water dog was getting too confusing? LET ME SPEND MY MONEY.

You're right. Well, not about most of the history. That was way off.

But the first part was right on point. Humans made money to make life less complicated (and to solidify and legitimize the power of the ruling elite, but that's a story for another day).[1] But then why is hanging on to it so hard? So stressful? So painful?

Believe it or not, quite a bit of it comes down to your brain. In this chapter, we're going to talk about the psychology of saving money and how to train yourself to hang on to your cash by developing better saving habits.

LOVE AND OTHER DRUGS

Humans love spending money because it makes us feel good. Clothes, cell phones, TVs, houses, cars, and for the Kardashians, private jets, are all status symbols. The bigger you buy, the cooler you are. And when it comes to human relations, cool is the most valuable currency out there.

But the good vibes and praise aren't only external. They're coming from your brain.

A 2019 study discovered "the common involvement of brain regions in both social and material reward anticipation."[2] Put another way, spending money (reward anticipation) puts us in the same cozy, warm, and positive feels as being in love (social anticipation). Those same parts of your brain that light up when you see a loved one are also activated when you see your favorite band's merch on the rack of your local vintage store.

We crave buying things the same way we crave human interaction. Which is seriously messed up and says as much about the world we've created as it does an individual person.

On the other hand, there's a reason not spending money on something you really, really, REALLY want hurts. Another study found a similar neural link between unforeseen expenses that eat into our spending money and the sensation of pain.[3]

And then there's the idea that humans are more likely to do something the more they are exposed to it. Say, for instance, you pass a billboard for McDonalds on your way to work in the morning. According to a tried and true marketing (and psychology) practice, you only need to hear or see a brand's message seven times before you take action and purchase the product.[4]

Now think about all of the advertisements out there for *stuff*. All of those influencers. Every label on a t-shirt. Now think about how many times *in your life* that you've seen an advertisement for saving money.

"We're bombarded by ads for products and shop in stores designed to encourage spending," one expert told NBC News in 2019. "At the same time, he added, "those without substantial assets receive much less encouragement from the marketplace to save regularly."[5]

With all of these obstacles in your way, is it really surprising that 40% of Americans don't have as much as $400 saved in case of an emergency? Or that only 7.5% of an average American's disposable income is saved every year?[6]

Here's what that looks like: the average US salary in 2023 is around $60,000 per year.[7] At a 22% tax rate, your net pay is $46,800, or about $3,900 per month. If half of that goes toward expenses (utilities, mortgage, groceries, insurance, etc.), you're left with $1,800 in gross income. Which means you're saving 7.5% of that amount, which is a grand total of $135 per month.

And, by the way, that's a generous figure. The average single individual has $3,405 in monthly expenses.[8] Taking that math, you're left with about $37.50 in savings if you only save 7.5%.

No wonder this is so stressful! Why save the $37.50 when you could just as easily put it toward literally anything else and wouldn't notice.

Okay, enough math. Let's get back to science, because the only way to fight the science going on in your brain is with, well, different science going on in your brain.

NECESSARY EVILS

It's impossible to have a conversation about saving and spending without also discussing what exactly you're spending money on. Generally, these purchases fall into two categories: needs and wants.

The definitions are fairly self-explanatory: a need is anything that satisfies a necessity of day-to-day living. Wants, on the other hand, is anything that could make our lives easier, but that we'd still be able to survive without.

The idea of "basic needs" is a concept also rooted in psychology. Psychologist Abraham Maslow divided up an individual's needs into five basic categories: physical or bodily, safety, love and belonging, esteem, and self-actualization.[9] Organized in a pyramid, humans need to satisfy each level of "need" before moving on to the next.

In other words: in order to reach the highest levels of fulfillment, you'll need to start by satisfying your lower-level physical and safety needs like shelter, food, and water.

Financially, these needs are your basic expenses. Often, you'll need to account for these expenses on a consistent basis—a housing payment and groceries, for example.

Think about it this way: how hard is it to do *anything* on an empty stomach? Or focus when a loved one is unhappy with you? When you aren't meeting your basic needs, you can't possibly hope to achieve your dreams.

But while not the case for every family, your housing payment, car insurance, groceries, and utilities are likely paid by your parents. As a result, it's not always easy to grasp every single need you'll face down the road. But they're coming.

So how can you prepare for calculating need-based expenses? We'll cover some techniques below (spoiler, you'll have to talk to your parents).

YOU HAVE TO DECIDE

You'll make plenty of purchases over the course of your life. Swiping a credit card is easy. What's harder is dividing those purchases into things you need versus things that you want.

If your parents pay for most of your needs, this is a great time to make mistakes. When you think about needs versus wants, don't worry about being right or wrong about something being a need versus a want. After all, there is a ton of grey area when it comes to these purchases. For instance, food is absolutely a need. And a large triple-topping pizza from Papa John's is food. Ergo, the $25 pizza is a need, right? Hmm . . . it may not feel like it.

That's what's important about this process: how you determine if something is a need versus a want. Ultimately, everyone is different, so your individual needs might be different than your friend's (remember the lesson about not comparing your finances to others?).

Your concern, right now, should be *why* something is a need versus a want. Having that conversation with yourself and being honest will save you heartache down the line, when your grown-up bills start piling up.

Also, it's okay if those needs and wants change. In fact, they should! If you still eat like a teenager when you're 30 (remember when those Flamin' Hot vending machine Cheetos were a need?) then you have more problems than just personal finance.

If you're truly honest with yourself, you may be surprised at how much money you actually save by simply cutting out extraneous expenses. In that sense, you aren't withholding anything you couldn't live without, which takes a bit of the pain out of saving money.

STEPS TO SAVING

Like with financial literacy, the only way to develop good saving habits is by constant practice. But where to even begin? For starters, always keep a goal in mind of something that you'd like to save up for. Humans are naturally goal-oriented, and while there's no immediate ecstasy hit that comes with saving like there is from spending, having something you're actively trying to work toward is an effective way to distract the brain.

Here are five steps, geared toward teens, suggested by Bank of America:[10]

1. **Find Your Magic Number.** How much is this thing you're saving for going to cost, anyway? The only way to start goal-oriented saving is by finding your magic number, or the total amount of the thing you want to buy.

Once you have that number in mind, subtract it from anything that you already have that you'd like to put towards the purchase. Maybe you have some lawn-mowing-money saved up. Or a few dollars from that aunt and uncle who never visit at Christmas but send cash in their place.

You can also get creative! Are there any deals coming up for your purchase? Any store-specific sales? Counting coupons isn't just for doomsday preppers on the TLC channel, okay? These will help lower your magic number and bring you closer to your ultimate goal.

2. **Know What to Set Aside.** Once you have that magic number, calculate in how many weeks you'd like to make the purchase. If it's the end of the school year and you're looking at buying a new pair of soccer cleats before the season starts in the fall, then you have around 12 weeks before your purchase. If you need a new bookbag for school next week, then you have, well, one week.

   Then divide the magic number by the number of weeks, and voila! You have the amount of money you need to set aside each week to reach your target. If your numbers seem impossible to reach, consider adjusting your timeline to give yourself a bit more leeway in accomplishing your goal.

3. **Save Without Thinking About It.** Here's where the science comes into play: turn your brain off. Or, at the very least, make it harder for your brain to access your money. If you don't have a bank account, consider opening one and having your parents deposit allowance or chores money in it. That way, you won't be as tempted to spend the cold hard cash burning a hole in your pocket every week when you cut the grass. This accesses a slightly sad feature of the human psyche: laziness.

   The simple truth is that the more steps you have to take to access your money, the less likely you will be to use it.

Similarly, there's a psychological concept called "nudge theory," in which indirect techniques are better at impacting one's behavior rather than a direct lesson.[11] In the classic example, a parent puts healthier food options at their kid's eye-level, lowering the junk food out of view, in order to get them to make healthier eating decisions. In essence, they are "nudging" the child to the right decision without forbidding junk food, a technique that is almost doomed to fail.

In this case, turning on automatic transfers into a savings account could be more effective than your parents simply telling you to save money. Instead of listening and *maybe* processing the information, you'll be able to see your money growing in action!

The best part? You don't have to think about it at all.

4. **Make Some Easy Spending Trade-Offs.** This is where knowing your needs versus wants will come in handy. The more spending trade-offs you can make, the quicker you'll get to your savings goal.

It doesn't have to be a seismic spending shift; small cutbacks here and there add up to huge savings. For instance, if you hit Chick-fil-a after school three times a week before play practice, you're probably spending around $30 per week. If we cut back on just *one* of those, going from $30 to $20, you'd save $260 in six months.

And if you decided to simply pack a snack from home, cutting out every Chick-fil-a trip, you'd save $780 in six months.

Continue tracking your spending over the course of your first month of saving. Try and find where your money is going and places where you can cut off the outflow of cash.

5. **Look for Ways to Make More Money.** Remember, you're not necessarily stuck at the same income-level for the entirety of your savings journey. Get creative about finding ways to earn more, like picking up an extra shift at work, doing more chores around the

house, or taking on a side-gig, like pet-sitting or, if you're 18, driving for DoorDash.

SMARTIES

Ultimately, the goal is not only to become a better saver, but a smarter spender as well. We don't want to eliminate *all* of the fun by saving everything—that might not be the path toward a healthy relationship with money, either.

Here are some tips to being a better spender:[12]

- **Comparison Shop**
  Chances are, multiple stores in town sell the same things. Walmart, Target, the Dollar Store, all generally sell the same basic necessities. Comparison shopping is making sure you're buying supplies from the place that sells it for the lowest price, ensuring you're not losing a few nickels here and there along the way.

- **Develop a Budget**
  Don't worry. The budget chapter is right . . . around . . . the corner . . .

- **Look for Alternatives to Spending**
  Boredom is a major contributor to mindless spending. You surf on Amazon or Instagram and before you know it, $150 is missing from your account. Be mindful about what you spend your money on, and always explore cheaper alternatives. For instance, rather than purchasing a new hardback book (which can go for $35), rent it for free from the library. It'll save you money, and storage space (we both know you aren't re-reading it).

- **Manage Your Credit Wisely**
  Stay tuned—we have a doozy of a chapter on credit for you!

THE ONE ABOUT SAVING

- **Record All Purchases**

  And who says accountants are only active in March? Keep a running log of everything you pay for. And seriously, *everything*. You'll see how quickly your purchases add up, while (hopefully) finding some ways to cut back and save.

- **Coupons!**

  Use them. Hunt for them. They are your friend. Side note: do *not* get into coupons just to buy things you won't use. There's no reason to have a garage full of coupon-bought trail mix if you're allergic to peanuts.

THE REAL WORLD . . . When trying to save money, don't be afraid to look for creative solutions to meet your goals. Here's a particularly fun solution from a real-life teenage saver:

"My dad opened the Bank of Dad in kindergarten. Each week, I could get a quarter now or 50 cents if I wanted to save it in the 'BOD.' Over time my allowance increased and I learned how to save up my money to buy the things I wanted. He had a whole setup inside a lunchbox with a calculator and an official log of all deposits and withdrawals. We could even deposit other money from babysitting or other odd jobs in the BOD. By the time I opened my first real bank account, I had over $1,000 saved up to deposit and have on my debit card. I've always been very money-conscious because of this and understood the value of saving for the future." [13]

If your parents offer you money as an allowance or even for chores, ask them about potentially letting your money earn "interest" by saving it and them adding an extra dollar to the earnings. As our real world example demonstrates, even the difference between a quarter and 50 cents can add up to thousands of dollars.

SUMMARY

Saving has as much do with your brain as it does your wallet. It makes perfect sense that money, (this thing humans invented to make life easier) brings us pain, because that's precisely what our brains tell us to feel.

But there are ways to take control of this psychological process. Dividing up needs and wants, shifting the mindset from one of restriction to one that is goal-oriented, and making the process as easy as possible helps to fight the brain's urge to spend, spend, spend.

Let's recap some easy mistakes made by teens when it comes to saving:

1. Setting Unrealistic Goals
Setting unrealistic goals is a surefire way to burnout. Start small to get the hang of things and prove to yourself that you can actually save. Going all-in is like quitting a habit cold turkey: it works for a few folks, but by and large you'll want to ease your way in.

Which is completely okay! Remember—you're a teenager. The goal is to start building these habits *early* so that by the time you're driving your own car covered by your own insurance through the Chick-fil-a drive-thru, you're plenty experienced.

Start off by simply trying to save money for a new t-shirt or book. Build your way up to more expensive purchases, like concert tickets (okay, *reasonably priced* concert tickets. General admission. Taylor Swift's Eras Tour may be fun, but you'll be mowing lawns for a *really* long time to save up for one of her shows).

2. Failing to Separate Needs and Wants

This mistake is less about dividing up purchases into clear-cut needs and wants and more about not thinking through *why* something is a want versus a need. The better able you are to explain how you determined if something is a need or a want shows that you've truly given thought to the difference.

3. Failing to Develop a Goal-Oriented Savings Mindset

Saving is hard. Saving with no end in sight is nearly impossible. Humans love setting goals for themselves, and saving is no different.

If you mindlessly stash money away, chances are you'll lose interest. And why shouldn't you? Other than self-discipline and that weird thing called "the future," you don't have any incentive. Instead, always be saving for *something*. Give yourself a tangible target: a trip, movie night, concert, clothes—anything. You'll find that saving for something is better than saving just to save.

4. Going Along With the Crowd

You're probably familiar with the bandwagon effect.[15] When everyone is excited about something, it's easy to get caught up in the frenzy. That's especially true of teenagers—whatever's trending immediately becomes a must-have.

And chances are, saving money is not going to be a popular decision. Just think back to our point about advertising: lots of requests to spend, few to save. It might be difficult to swim against the current, but then again, cargo pants were all the rave once. And Phiten necklaces. And Justin Bieber's haircut.

Point is, some trends just aren't worth following.

(continued) SUMMARY

5. Putting Things Off for the Future

This is a problem that plagues teens and adults alike: only saving money when you think you can.[16] But when you're a teen (and presumably not making thousands of dollars in salary every year), even saving $10 can be a massive chunk of change. This makes it easy to put off saving until down the line, when you think you'll have more money to set aside.

Here's the problem: if you don't develop those saving habits early, you never will. It will *always* be hard getting started to save, whether you're making $7.50 an hour scooping ice cream or the c-suite exec in charge of supplying the shop with soft serve.

EXERCISE

Now it's your turn to practice what you've learned in this chapter. Here are some ideas to get you going:

Set Up Auto-Draft Into a Saving Account
The easiest way to save is when you don't have to think about it. Ask your parents to help you set up a bank account, if you don't have one. Then see if they would be willing to directly deposit money into your account, or take a slice off and deposit it into a savings account. Alternatively, you can set up a separate savings account that automatically pulls from your checking account each month.

BEGIN BY . . . Research different savings accounts offered by your bank, and compare interest rates.

Develop Three Savings Goals
This one's easy. What are three things you'd like to purchase with your own money? They can be purchases you want to make soon, as in a few weeks. On the other hand, you could think of longer-term purchases that might take several months or even years, like a car.

Figure out how much each of those three goals will cost and map out ways to start saving today.

BEGIN BY . . . Starting small. The reason for having three goals is so that you don't set your sights too high on the first one. Is there a particular sweatshirt you have your eye on? A movie you want to see? Keep in mind, building good habits usually starts with baby steps.

(continued) EXERCISE

Conduct a Price Comparison

Think about a purchase your family makes every month. Ask your parents how much that individual item costs every time they purchase it. Also ask how often they purchase it, so that you can get a sense for how much that item costs per year.

Then, hop online and see if the same item is cheaper anywhere else. Maybe another store in town offers a few cents off, or even an online retailer has a long-term purchasing deal. Amazon, for instance, generally knocks down some prices for household goods in the event you opt-in to automatic deliveries every so often.

Then, take your findings to your parents and wow them with all of the money they could save every year!

BEGIN BY . . . Researching paper towels. They are a) way more expensive than you might think, b) a recurring purchase, and c) offer many different varieties to choose from. Chances are, you can find a cheaper alternative somewhere!

ENDNOTES

1. Lanchester, Jr. (2019, July 29). The Invention of Money. *The New Yorker*. https://www.newyorker.com/magazine/2019/08/05/the-invention-of-money

2. Gu, R., Huang, W., Camilleri, J., Xu, P., Wei, P., Eickhoff, S. B., & Feng, C. (2019). Love is analogous to money in human brain: Coordinate-based and functional connectivity meta-analyses of social and monetary reward anticipation. Neuroscience and biobehavioral reviews, 100, 108–128. https://doi.org/10.1016/j.neubiorev.2019.02.017

3. Knutson, B., Rick, S., Wimmer, G. E., Prelec, D., & Loewenstein, G. (2007). Neural predictors of purchases. *Neuron, 53*(1), 147–156. https://doi.org/10.1016/j.neuron.2006.11.010

4. Kruse, K. (2021, September 29). *Rule of 7: How Social Media Crushes Old School Marketing.* Kruse Control. https://www.krusecontrolinc.com/rule-of-7-how-social-media-crushes-old-school-marketing-2021/#:~:text=The%20Marketing%20Rule%20of%207,movie%20industry%20in%20the%201930s.

5. Nova, A. (2019, May 1). *You really want to save money but aren't. The reason may surprise you.* NBC News. https://www.nbcnews.com/better/lifestyle/you-really-want-save-money-aren-t-reason-why-may-ncna1000306?ref=finco-services.ghost.io

6. Ibid.

7. Wong, B. (2023, July 17). Average Salary By State in 2023. *Forbes.* https://www.forbes.com/advisor/business/average-salary-by-state/

8. Flynn, J. (2023, April 4). *20+ AVERAGE MONTHLY EXPENSE STATISTICS [2023]: AVERAGE HOUSEHOLD SPENDING IN AMERICA.* Zippia. https://www.zippia.com/advice/average-monthly-expenses/#:~:text=The%20average%20individual%20spends%2055,compared%20to%20families%20and%20households.

9. Schultz, K. (n.d.) *Needs and Wants: Definition, Difference, and Examples.* Berkeley Well-Being Institute. https://www.berkeleywellbeing.com/needs-and-wants.html

10. Bank of America (n.d.). *How to Save Money as a Teenager.* https://bettermoneyhabits.bankofamerica.com/en/saving-budgeting/saving-money-as-a-teenager

11. Seacoast Bank. (n.d.). *The Psychology of Saving Money.* https://www.seacoastbank.com/resource-center/blog/saving-money-psychology

12. SOCU. (2021, July 21). *What Does It Mean to Be a Smart Spender?* https://www.socu.com/blog/teen-smart-spending

13. Liscomb, M. (2021, June 17). *Parents Are Sharing How They Teach Kids About Money And I Honestly Learned From Them Too.* Buzzfeed. Reprinted with permission.

14. *New York Times.* (2004, November 14). Needs vs Wants. https://www.nytimes.com/2004/11/14/opinion/business/needs-vs-wants-614343.html

15. Seacoast Bank. *Psychology.*

16. Bruehl, E. (2021, June 15). *The Psychology of Money: Saving and Spending Habits.* Current. https://current.com/blog/the-psychology-of-money-saving-and-spending-habits/

Chapter 3

BALLIN' ON A BUDGET

"It takes as much energy to wish as it does to plan."
  —Eleanor Roosevelt

"Happiness is not in the mere possession of money; it lies in the joy of achievement, in the thrill of creative effort."
  —Franklin D. Roosevelt

Webster's dictionary defines budgeting as "to jump from a height while attached to an elasticized cord."[1]

Wait a second. No. Sorry, that's the definition of *bungee* jumping. No, no, budgeting sounds like something way scarier and far more nauseating: "a plan for the coordination of resources and expenditures."[2] Gross. Shivers down the spine incoming.

Unfortunately, as annoying, frustrating, and constraining as a budget might feel, we have to talk about it. Because going through life without at least some sort of a budget is like bungee jumping without the elasticized cord. It's a freefall.

A budget doesn't mean you can't enjoy yourself. In the wise words of every parent of every horror movie involving a possessed doll: it's there to be your friend! Think about it like, well, bungee jumping: you can still experience the thrill of plummeting several stories with the peace of mind that you've planned it out in advance and have a protective mechanism in place.

Your budget is your protection. It's not a cage; it's a shield. In this chapter, you'll learn different budgeting strategies and how to create a budgeting plan.

BASICS

But before diving in, let's make sure you're on the same page about what exactly a budget looks like, because depending on what your goals are (and how you actually use the word "budget,") the specifics can vary.

First and foremost, a budget (in its noun form) is, in its most basic form, a spending plan. You take however much you earn and put it in a column and however much you spend (or plan to spend) and put it in another column.

You may wish to write it all out by hand, or use a tool like Microsoft Excel or a specially designed budgeting app to keep everything in order.

The purpose behind a budget is simple: take control of your money.[3] Think back to our bungee jumping example. It's easy to go flying off the edge, spending willy-nilly, completely out of control. But without an idea of how much money you make, it's easy to spend *more money* than you make, the financial equivalent of splatting on the pavement.

A budget isn't meant to deprive you of the things you love, either. Remember the mindset shift from the chapter on savings? Budgeting works the same way: it's a tool to be used to empower you to make the right financial decisions.

Here are just a few reasons why budgeting is crucial:

- **Get to Know Your Money**
  We're all about developing a positive relationship to money. By tracking all of your expenses and income in a budget, you can clearly see the amount of money at your disposal every month. It makes adjusting your spending even easier: you'll find subscriptions you no longer use but forgot to cancel, you'll see how much (or little!) you spend on eating out, etc.

- **The Future**
  Emergencies happen. When you set a budget, you can carve out an entire portion of it as an "emergency fund" designed to get you through the difficult time. A budget also helps you create a game plan to save up for future positive goals, like retirement or a swanky European getaway.

- **Debt**
  Yes, a budget is designed to keep you from overspending, or accruing debt. But even if you're already in debt (from, say, student loans), a budget will keep you on track to meet monthly payments. Who knows, it might even offer ways to pay down your debts quicker than you even realize!

- **Detox**
  Over 50% of American adults say money contributes to added stress. Nearly one in three say money stresses them out *daily*.[4] While budgeting isn't a stand-in for something like therapy, it takes some of the unknown out of your financial future. It puts you back in control of your money, rather than the other way around.

PICKING YOUR STRATEGY

Every budget is different. That's the idea—everyone's financial situation is a little different, so the money allocated to different expenses naturally varies. But generally, you can boil most budgets down into three types: "pay yourself first," "zero-based budgeting," and the "50/30/20 rule."[5]

Here's a breakdown:

NAME	HOW IT WORKS	PROS	CONS
Pay Yourself First	You immediately put a set amount of money (or percentage of your paycheck) into savings	Ideal when saving for big future events, like a trip, wedding, or retirement Allows for flexibility, especially if your salary isn't set each month	Lack of structure after adding money to savings Can be tempting to aggressively save, leaving less money for later expenses
Zero-Based Budgeting	Estimate the total number of expenses, splitting your income up until you have zero left over	Accounting for every single dollar in your budget Ease and uniformity	Requires constant supervision as income levels and expenses change Leaves little wiggle-room during the month for unanticipated expenses
50/30/20	Allocate 50% of your income for necessary expenses (needs), 30% for other expenses (wants), and 20% for savings	An easy framework to work from Ensures you cover each and every anticipated expense	A little more rigid, which isn't ideal for fluctuating salaries

So which is the best for teens? It depends on your individual financial situation. But by and large, the 50/30/20 method is a tried and true method that will start you thinking about allocating money to all three categories.

In addition, it encompasses several of the lessons you've learned already: dividing between needs and wants, mindful saving, and the like.

If you do go the 50/30/20 route, be sure to stay flexible. Those percentages are guideposts and shouldn't be set in stone each and every month. For instance, you may have a month with more necessary expenses (like, if you run out of paper towels and other household necessities). In that case, you may need to allocate 55% of your budget to necessary expenses and less to your other two. It's okay to mix things up and adapt based on your individual situation.

THE GAME PLAN

With your specific budgeting strategy in hand, it's time to set up an actual plan. After all, those budgets are just the framework that give this process some form. But to actually flesh it out, you'll need a road map. Here's how:

Calculate your income

This step is probably the most obvious. If you're going to budget the right way, you need to know how much you're bringing in each month.

> SIDE NOTE—*Most budgets are monthly since that's how salaries are often paid out. But you can also set up weekly, bi-monthly, or yearly budgets, but those might be harder to maintain.*

Remember, you aren't taking your gross pay—chances are a good chunk of that is being cut out and sent to the government as taxes. Instead, calculate your income's net pay, or the amount you receive after taxes are taken out. If your income varies from month to month, then go back six months and take the average. That should give you a good estimate for your monthly income, even if it isn't set in stone.

Track your spending

It's impossible to overstate how important this step is. Unless you deliberately go through each of your monthly expenses, you'll never be able to accurately budget. Don't ballpark things, don't leave them up to chance, and don't guesstimate. The only way to know exactly how much things cost is by reviewing the tape.

And don't just go back and track spending over the last month. Go back over the last six months. Maybe the last *year*. For instance, if you get ice cream every month in the summer, chances are that expense category will be misleadingly small in December. As a result, you may not properly budget for that category, which means less ice cream when the summer rolls back around.

Here's how to accurately track your spending:[6]

1. **Set Up Your Account:** If you already have a bank account, awesome. You're ahead of the game. If you don't have one, that's okay, too! But get one ASAP. It will be significantly easier to track your spending when it's all in one place, your bank statement. Without an account, you'll be left hunting for receipts in the trash can for cash purchases. And that stinks, in more ways than one

2. **Check Your Accounts Regularly:** Give that account some love! Don't ignore it! With banking apps, it's possible to see how much money you have in real time. This will help you adjust your spending, also in real time.

3. **Categorize Your Spending:** After some time has passed, you'll start amassing a nice spending record. At this point, it's time to categorize those purchases. If you're going with the 50/30/20 method, split everything into necessary expenses (needs like food, shelter, etc,), other expenses (wants like entertainment, clothes, etc.), and anything that goes toward savings or debt repayment (like loans, retirement, etc.).

This is the heart of your budget. Take it seriously.

Set realistic goals

Remember this mistake from last chapter? Setting unrealistic goals is how burnout starts. That's not to say you shouldn't budget aggressively. But don't go overboard right out of the gate and remember that you've likely grown accustomed to a certain lifestyle without a budget. If your goals severely restrict that lifestyle, there's a chance you'll grow resentful of the budget and quit before you even get started.

Realistic budgeting goals are those that let you live the same lifestyle (unless drastic changes are needed) while also satisfying whatever reasons you have for starting the budget in the first place. Striking the right balance comes with time, so don't get discouraged if things don't work out right away!

Adjust your spending to stay on budget
and review your budget regularly

Maybe your first budget doesn't quite work out on a month-to-month basis. Maybe you're finding that you spend more money than you expected when you set up your budget. Maybe you're spending less.

Either way, it's important to adjust your budget according to how you actually live and spend. In addition, if you have a temporary expense on the horizon, you can get ahead of it by adjusting your budget to meet that expenditure.

Say, for instance, your favorite band is coming to town. To save for that concert (in accordance with what you learned from last chapter), you may move some things around in your budget to make room for the tickets. That probably means allocating less money for Starbucks trips or cutting back on drive-thru runs.

Then, once the concert has come and gone and your voice is back, you can reset your budget. Coffee and drive-thru runs are back!

Remember, the point of your budget is to give yourself some ease of mind. Not following your budget is only going to add stress to your plate. If that's the case, simply revisit your budget and make the proper adjustment so that your plan reflects your reality.

And, since you are a teen and most likely your expenses are covered by your parents, keep in mind that this is all just practice. This is the time to make budgeting mistakes, so that when you have to set aside money for things like insurance and mortgages you're a seasoned pro.

Ultimately, as long as you're not overdrawing your account, most budgeting errors are possible to come back from as a teenager. That said, those personal finance habits only develop with constant focus and attention. Don't use the low stakes as an opportunity to cut corners or you'll do the exact same when the stakes are higher.

HIT THE APP STORE

Don't forget to use technology to your advantage. Back in the day, we had to budget by hand, writing out each and every expense on paper.

But there are plenty of apps out there that make budgeting a breeze. Some, link Mint, actually link to your bank account and track your current spending habits for you, so you get a rough idea of areas to potentially cut back. If you're going with the Zero-Based Budgeting, then the YNAB app is tough to beat, as it allocates every cent you earn for you. Finally, options like GoodBudget, Every Dollar, and PocketGuard are great budget-based apps, as well.

THE REAL WORLD . . . One of the best resources to develop your budgeting habits are your parents. Here are a few examples of how teens (and families) are building good budgeting habits early:[7] *"Next year, my son will be able to leave school to buy lunch. I've told him what our weekly budget for his lunches is and I will put him in charge of the money. He can tell me what to get from the grocery store or he can buy from the cafeteria or the pizza place nearby, but whatever money from his weekly budget he doesn't spend, he can keep.*

My goal is to get him thinking about budgeting early and understanding that you can make trade-offs. He can spend more on food and have less extra to spend, or vice versa like a mini, low-stakes version of what he'll do later as an adult.

We also talk with both kids about what things cost and how we budget the family's money. They know we're spending more for our mortgage because we wanted a bit more space, that we save some money every month for retirement and other needs, and what it costs to eat a home cooked meal versus a restaurant meal."

Sure, the stakes might be low. But the difference between a PB&J and a meat lovers supreme pizza is huge. Which is why it's unsurprising that early budgeting tends to revolve around the cheesy, marinara-y goodness: *"[W]hen I was a kid, my mom would write a check worth $2 a day for the month for me to deposit into my "school lunch account" or whatever. I could use it however I wanted — only spend $1 today so I could spend $3 tomorrow, etc. If I ran out of money before the end of the month, I'd have to bring lunch from home. That wasn't ideal because I could get pizza at school. Learning to budget early truly helps later in life."*

SUMMARY

A budget is your friend. Repeat that: a budget is your friend. Yes, it's often thought of as a stressor, a constraint, and a jail.

But done the right way, a budget is designed to liberate you from the stress associated with blindly spending money. If you take these steps seriously, you'll begin forming new habits and a new routine with your money. Yes, it may require a few changes to your lifestyle, but eventually, those changes will become the new norm.

Here are some mistakes teens often make when making up their budget:

1. Failing to Take it Seriously
Many teens try to get away with ballparking their monthly expenses. This is an example of not taking your budget seriously. Unless you go through the process of working out your actual expenses on a monthly basis, your budget will be inaccurate and you will be less likely to go through with the entire process.

2. Quitting or Burning Out
Remember the problem associated with setting unrealistic expectations? Inevitably, if you feel like your budget isn't working, you're more likely to simply quit. Ditto if you bite off more than you can chew right off the bat. Just like with saving, start small and work your way up.

3. Failing to Adjust
Of course, the opposite of quitting is adjusting. But so many teens fail to adjust their budget after making it the first time. Remember that your budget is meant to meet your individual needs and that those needs change

frequently. Think about the person you were just a year ago. Would that person have the same budget as the refined contributor to society you are now one year later? No! Adjust your budget accordingly.

4. Feeling Controlled By Your Budget
If one end of the spectrum is not taking your budget seriously enough, the other is feeling controlled by it. This is especially dangerous with the 50/30/20 method, where you may feel compelled to meet those exact percentages each and every month.

This is bound to add stress to your financial situation, the very thing a budget is designed to alleviate. If you don't hit exactly 50% in a given month, that's okay. As long as you're close, you're doing the right thing.

5. Choosing the Wrong Budget
While we recommend the 50/30/20 budget for its ease of use, the "pay yourself first" and "zero-based budgeting" are also excellent options and might be a better fit given your individual situation. For instance, if you have significant savings goals or debt, you may want to pay yourself first to address those needs. Or if you have a hard and fast income each week or month, the zero-based budget might be for you.

Budgets, like dogs, are best when they reflect the individuals that own them.

EXERCISE

Perhaps the most obvious exercise here is to set up your own budget. But let's assume that you'll actually do that. With that in mind, here are a few exercises that will help bolster your budget-making abilities:

Talk to Your Parents

Chances are, your parents have budgeted before. Even if they haven't there's probably a learning lesson in there too.

BEGIN BY . . . Asking your parents how they budgeted for you. Literally. Having a child is a massive expense, requiring money for hospital bills, clothes, diapers, food, formula, day care, and so on. What changes to their pre-existing budget did they have to make? Did they pick up more shifts at work?

Research Emergencies

Not to get all grim here, but emergencies happen. Broken arms, flooded basements, all of them capable of striking at any time. As a teenager, you might not fully grasp the importance of having an emergency fund allocated as part of your budget.

But what happens when you leave your summer job because you can't squeeze it into the school year, between class, sports, and homework? Suddenly your money is gone. You may want to have some money saved up so that you don't have to immediately cut back on all the fun activities you could afford when you had a consistent income.

BEGIN BY. . . Thinking about how different your lifestyle would be if you suddenly lost your source of income. What could you still afford? How long could you afford to eat out? Purchase gas?

ENDNOTES

1. Merriam-Webster. (n.d.). *Bungee.* https://www.merriam-webster.com/dictionary/bungee%20jump

2. Merriam-Webster. (n.d.). *Budget.* https://www.merriam-webster.com/dictionary/budget

3. Scwhann, L. (2023, May 16). *What is a budget?* NerdWallet. https://www.nerdwallet.com/article/finance/what-is-a-budget

4. Bennett, R. (2023, June 26). *Most Americans are significantly stressed about money — here's how it varies by demographic.* BankRate. https://www.bankrate.com/banking/money-and-financial-stress-statistics/#:~:text=How%20common%20is%20financial%20stress,health%2C%20including%20by%20causing%20stress.

5. Mint. (2021, March 29). *Budgeting for Teens: 14 Tips for Growing Your Money Young.* https://mint.intuit.com/blog/budgeting/budgeting-for-teens/

6. Rockwood, K. (2020, September 25). *Tracking Your Finances: A Guide for Teens.* Step. https://step.com/money-101/post/tracking-your-finances-a-guide-for-teens Reprinted with permission.

7. Liscomb. *Parents are Sharing.* Reprinted with permission.

Chapter 4

STASH YOUR CASH

Many people take no care of their money till they come nearly to the end of it, and others do just the same with their time.
—Johann Wolfgang von Goethe

If we command our wealth, we shall be rich and free. If our wealth commands us, we are poor indeed.
—Edmund Burke

At this point, we've talked a lot about how to spend money wisely. Where do you put it? How do you divvy it up? But . . . we're sort of missing an obvious step: how to get your hands on that cash.

This can be a daunting task, right? What with all those pesky "child labor laws" keeping you from building your resume before age 14? And then there's homework, school sports, club sports, band practice, homework, chorus rehearsal, and let's not forget: homework. When eight hours of your life is taken up by school, when is there time for anything else?

That's where this chapter comes in. In it, we will tackle how teens can get their first job, which means making a first paycheck. And then, with that paycheck in hand, we'll chat about different bank accounts and how to pick the right one for your needs.

Let's dive in!

FIRST THINGS FIRST . . .

It doesn't matter if you are 14 or 44; getting a new job is scary. It can feel challenging. Where do you even begin? And, for the record, your parents come home at the end of the day exhausted with a few more bags under their eyes . . . are we really sure this is even *smart*?

The truth is, no. Our system is flawed for many reasons, but unfortunately, for the time being, it is *our system*. We have to play by its rules.

But that doesn't mean you can't take steps to make the most of a flawed system. Let's start with a biggie: burnout.

Burnout is real. During the COVID-19 pandemic, upwards of 52% of surveyed adults reported feeling a sense of burnout associated with their work.[1]

Yeah, but those are adults doing adult jobs. True. Yes. Correct. But just like building strong financial skills now will help you in the future, developing a positive relationship with your work will also help combat burnout down the road.

Chances are, you won't feel the same existential dread that some adults do going to work every day (OK, you may feel that way about school). But, regardless of what you do, there will be days where you just. Don't. Want to.

One step you can begin taking now as a teen is to focus on your *why*. Why do you want a job? What are your goals in getting it? It's not that different than asking yourself *why* you want to budget or *what* you want to save up for—developing a *why* when it comes to a job will give you that extra boost before clocking in.

And it will keep the burnout monsters away. "Getting into the practice of reminding yourself why you chose your career in the first place is an important step in learning to love your job again," advises one clinical psychologist. "Trying to understand the driving force behind why you chose your career can help facilitate meaning and fulfillment in your job."[2]

Let's take that quote and swap out words like "career" for "job." While you probably aren't choosing a *career* in your teens (you shouldn't), you should absolutely find a job that fits with your goals.

BENEFITS ON BENEFITS

While making money is likely top of mind when getting a new job, there are a few more benefits worth considering. For starters, your first job helps you build confidence. Whenever you start working, you're inevitably trying something new for the first time. The confidence you pick up from succeeding at something for the first time can be used as momentum for any other activity you're engaged in.

In addition, just *getting* a job can feel like the hard part. Having someone trust you with their business is like saying they believe in you, they're confident in you.

In addition, you pick up invaluable work experience. This is helpful when trying to get your next job, but also with college applications. Work experience sends a signal to colleges that an applicant is trustworthy, responsible, and willing to work for their goals.

"Even a miserable job flipping burgers or washing dishes has value on your application," says ThoughtCo. "You've learned to be responsible, to serve others before yourself, and to make sacrifices to meet your long-term goals. Work experience and maturity tend to go hand-in-hand."[3]

TEENS + JOBS = $$$

For the most part, your *why* for getting a job as a teen will be to add a little extra spending money to your wallet. That's a given. But you may also want a job that is only part-time so that you can balance your other activities. If you have a food allergy, you may want a job that doesn't require working with said food. If you don't have reliable transportation, you might want a job that is within walking or biking distance, or along a bus route.

Here are several excellent job ideas for teens that have been vetted by the online banking service Copper:[4]

- **Retail**

  Do you spend all day combing through racks of clothes? Have a go-to shop whenever you need a fresh fit? Retail might be for you. You'll get excellent customer service experience, you'll just have to practice your *"Can I help you find anything?"* voice. Oh—and you'll probably get an employee discount, which isn't a bad perk, either.

- **Cafés and Bakeries**

  Does your Bath and Body Works candle smell like fresh bread and coffee grounds? Love cozy vibes? Have your friends' Starbucks order memorized (one shot cold foam, two pumps caramel, hold the ice, a drizzle of pumpkin spice)? Then why not try your hand at a bakery or coffee shop? You'll pick up some excellent people skills, and, hey, the look on a customer's face when they get their first cup of Joe in the morning is about as rewarding as it gets.

- **Restaurants**

  Maybe you're someone who wants to go above and beyond and make more than a low starting salary. As an adult, you'll be perfect for a commission-based job. But as a teen, you might find your start working for a restaurant. The starting pay isn't awesome (generally lower than minimum wage), but you'll be working for tips, which (at least to some extent) is governed by the quality of your service. You might also find work as a busser or host if working the floor isn't your thing (look, it makes sense—the food is just too enticing not to eat).

- **Friends and Family**
Finally, don't be afraid to hit up a friend or family member, especially if they own their own business. You'll have a built-in, pre-existing relationship with the boss, which always comes in handy down the line if you want to take on more responsibility.

   These are some traditional teen jobs. Which is awesome! But thanks to the Internet, teens have way more opportunities to make money now than ever before! Here are a few 21st-century options:

   - Online Survey Responder
   - Blogger
   - YouTuber
   - Social Media Manager
   - Operate an Etsy Marketplace
   - Social Media Influencer

Once you've settled on a job, you'll want to show up to an interview or first day prepared. Here are a few tips to get you started off on the right foot:

- **Create a Resume**
A resume is a document that includes all of your relevant work experience up to that point. *Wait, I'm a teen. I have no work experience.* Probably so. *THEN HOW DO I MAKE A RESUME?!*

   Fair question. Think about yourself, though. What have you done that shows an employer your trustworthiness? Have you held any positions in school clubs? That requires at least some faith in your abilities (beyond the vote just being a popularity contest). Maybe you were club treasurer—that means you've been entrusted to keep up with a club's money! That's a huge responsibility!

   Or maybe you play a team sport. In order to do so, you'll have to have at least *some* interpersonal skills. It means you work well in a team environment. You know how to deal with *people*. Did you crush your school's spelling bee? Then chances are you're one who isn't afraid of spending time to learn something the right way, which employers love. Ditto for any other school competition, like a science fair. In both cases, you've demonstrated a way to separate yourself from a field of competitors. Think about what made you succeed, like strong time management skills. Time management is like catnip to employers: they all absolutely love it.

You've probably been picking up skills along the way and never even realized it. But a little critical thinking will probably reveal some strengths you didn't even know you had.

- **Know the Law and Your Rights**
  In the United States, no one under the age of 14 is allowed to work, period.[5] Until you're 16, you'll only be allowed to work under certain conditions. Jobs that are too dangerous (like in a coal mine or a welding torch) or with prohibited goods (like alcohol) are also off-limits for minors, as well.

  In addition, the Youth Minimum Wage is less than that of an adult worker.[6] *But*, that is a *temporary* rule: after 90 days, the temporary minor's minimum wage of $4.25/hour goes up to the federally-mandated $7.25/hour. So, if you've been working somewhere longer than 90 days, you're entitled to the higher amount.

- **Taxes**
  Lastly, keep in mind that if you make more than $12,550 per year with your job, you'll be required to pay taxes on your income.[7] Sometimes, those taxes will be automatically taken out when you get paid (and then you'll be reimbursed at the tax deadline if your salary never crossed the $12,500 threshold). In other cases, your taxes will *not* be taken out beforehand, and you'll be mailed your income information around tax time for use to fill out your taxes. If that's the case, you probably won't be getting a reimbursement, because no money was taken out for taxes in the first place!

  Also, keep this in mind—teens are tax exempt below that $12,550 threshold. And you'd have to work something like 14 hours per week in a state with a $14 minimum wage in order to get to $12,550. Given the already jam-packed high school schedule, a 14 hour work week probably isn't happening.

After a few weeks, you'll likely get your first paycheck. Woohoo! Take a second to relish that feeling. Money in your hand.

And now, it's time. The moment you've been waiting for. A place cherished by accountants, athletes, and Cardi B alike: the bank.

BANKING BASICS

So you walk into a bank. Everything seems pretty normal, right? Maybe you've been to one before. Maybe you've *even* been given a lollipop by the nice tellers.

Well, not today. Because lollipops are for kids who play with Monopoly money (kidding—you should absolutely ask for a victory lollipop after your first personal banking experience).

But it's true that by walking into that bank (or getting on an app), you're taking a concrete step forward into a future of financial power. But as you get closer to the teller's window, your feet might start feeling like concrete. A checking or savings account? A money market? *Huh*?

Don't run out of the bank. Don't sweat. Don't put your money under your mattress. Take a deep breath. And read on.

DEEP POCKETS, DE-POSITS

Let's start at square one: deposits. A deposit is any money that you put into your account. There are three types of deposits: cash, check, and direct.

Remember that feeling of having your paycheck in hand? Well . . . that was a bit of a lie. Most jobs drop your paycheck into your bank account via direct deposit. But as a teen, it's not uncommon to work jobs where you get paid in cash or via check from your employer.

If that's the case, you'll have to take your cash or check to the bank to deposit into your account. Alternatively, most banking apps let you snap a picture of a check and deposit it right into your account.

The key difference is how quickly you'll have access to the money. In the case of direct deposit and checks, it might take a day or two for the money to *actually* hit your account. But with cash, as soon as you deposit the money, you can use it.

But in order to use it, you'll need an account.

COUNTING YOUR ACCOUNTS

When you make a deposit, the money goes into a banking account. There are three general types: savings, checking, and investment account.[8]

A checking account is probably the most basic account you can get. There are no limits to the amount of transactions you can make and no restrictions to accessing your money. The flip side? Your money won't add any interest—it just sits there.

A savings account, on the other hand, is designed as a safe space for your savings goals. In order to keep you on track, banks typically limit the number of transactions you can make from these accounts (usually six max). Also, it's not uncommon for banks to have very low-interest rates on these accounts so that whatever you have in your account grows over time. Keep in mind—this is an extremely low-interest rate, so this type of account is best used for short-term savings goals.

Finally, we get to investment accounts. These are for your long-term savings goals, as they earn much higher interest than savings accounts. But like savings accounts, an investment account limits the number of transactions you can make on a monthly basis.

One of the most common investment accounts is a money market account. With higher interest rates and predictable yields, money market accounts are an excellent option to earn money over time. The key difference is that a money market might require a higher minimum balance in the account in order to keep it active.[9]

So you have your paycheck, you have your deposit set up, and you have your account of choice (and, hopefully, a budget!). Now it's time to spend that money! And for that, you'll need a card.

CARD SHARK

Not all banking cards are made equally. You're probably familiar with the two types: credit and debit cards, but maybe a bit fuzzier about how they work.

A debit card is a card attached to your checking account. You can only use what's in the checking account, although in some cases, banks allow for overdraft (which is when you spend *more* than what you have in a checking account). If that were to happen, you would have to pay a serious penalty. And in many cases, banks *let* teens overdraft on purpose, just to get the overdraft fee. That's a red flag, and not a bank you want to do business with!

A credit card, on the other hand, lets you spend as much money as you want in the present (or, as much as the card's credit limit allows), with the expectation that you'll pay it off before the end of a billing period (almost always one month). If you don't pay off the balance before the end of the pay period, that money stays in your account and earns interest, meaning you'll end up paying off *more* than you initially spent on the card. In addition, failing to pay off your credit card's balance could negatively affect your credit score.

The amount of interest on a credit card is called the annual percentage rate (APR). Generally, an APR of around 20% is considered "good."[10] Keep this in mind: APR is a *yearly* interest rate. So, while you may have to make *monthly* payments, you won't be paying 20% in interest on unpaid credit card debt every month. Rather, APR reflects the accumulated amount of interest charged on any unpaid debt at the end of the year.[11]

Confused yet? Here's how it works: let's say you spend $120 in a month on your credit card, but only make a $20 payment, leaving you with $100 in your account. If you didn't use the card for the rest of the year, an additional $20 in interest that you would be required to pay would be added to your account.

We'll dive into credit and credit scores in the next chapter. But for now, just know that the same rule for debit cards should apply for credit cards: never spend more than you have or intend to make by the end of the pay period.

You might also have something called a "prepaid debit card," which is essentially like a reloadable gift card. With this card, you're not allowed to overdraft *at all*, which is great for those who tend to go a little overboard on spending. You'll learn how to reign it in *and* won't be penalized for spending more than you have (because . . . you can't).

BANK STATEMENTS

At the end of the pay period, you'll get a handy letter either in the mail or through your email called a bank statement.

A bank statement keeps track of all of your expenditures in a given month on a given card. It's an excellent way to track your spending when trying to, say, make a budget! In many cases, the statement will divvy up your account by income and expenses, so you can get a pretty good idea of where your spending habits are.

The bank statement will also include the date by which you must pay off your credit card. Generally, you have one month after a statement goes out to pay off the card.

YOU TRY IT NOW

At the end of each chapter, you get a series of exercises designed to get you practicing what you've learned. Don't worry, that's not changing—there will still be a few practice pointers.

But . . . opening a bank account can be a little intimidating, so we're going to walk through the steps now so you have a how-to guide to take some of the edge off:

STEP ONE: Find the right account for you

Remember how important planning is to this *entire* personal finance process? The same is true of banking. You'll want to do your homework and plan out the right account for you.[12] Here's a handy breakdown of which account might be best for you depending on your situation:

TYPE OF ACCOUNT	BEST FOR
Checking	Teens with reliable incomes/jobs
Savings	Teens who are just beginning the job hunt and don't yet have a reliable source of income
Prepaid Debit Card	Those wanting to learn how to manage their money effectively and those who tend to overspend
Investment Accounts	Teens interested in long-term saving; also useful for parents, who can make investment decisions on behalf of the teen while also keeping the account in the teen's name

At this phase, you'll also want to research any fees associated with an account. Are there withdrawal fees? ATM fees? Credit limits? What's the credit card's APR? For a prepaid debit card, are there reload fees associated with putting money in an account?

Asking (and answering) questions will also help you make the right decision about an account.

STEP TWO: Applications

After deciding which account to set up, you'll have to fill out an application. Unless you're over 18, this process will most likely have to be completed with a parent or guardian, who will share custody of the account with you.

In some cases, a bank might make you come in person and file the application. In other cases, you can file the application from a laptop or phone.

Either way, you'll need to have some personal info handy. So if you're doing this from home, make sure your connection is safe and secure before handing over your Social Security Number, name, date of birth, and a photo of your driver's license or ID. Carefully review the application before hitting submit so that everything is on point.

After the 10-15 minutes it takes to complete the application, you wait.

And wait.

And wait.

What's the holdup? During this process, the bank is doing a check on your banking history (if applicable) as well as your parent or guardian's. They want to know that, in case you do happen to go hard online shopping or drop a bit too much on concert tickets, they'll get their money back.

If you're opening a credit card, keep in mind that you'll likely need at least *some* credit history in order for your application to go through. Online sites like Credit Karma will help you check your credit score for free while also suggesting credit cards based on your history and score.

STEP THREE: Funding your account

Woohoo! You did it! Assuming your application was accepted, you're all ready to get started. To fully activate your account, you'll need to make a minimum deposit (usually between $25 and $100).[13]

Then, once you receive your debit card (if opening a checking account) or credit card (if opening a line of credit), you'll need to activate the card. This process is fairly straightforward and can be done over the phone or online. Your card will come with activation instructions, and until the card is activated, it's about as useful as studying for an algebra test during your lunch period before the exam. Which is to say, it's not useful at all.

Go ahead and download your bank's app on your phone. This will give you instant access to your accounts and balance information.

STEP FOUR: Setting up direct deposit

Once you have your account, you can set up direct deposit through your work, if they offer it. You'll need to supply your employer with your routing and account numbers and the address associated with the account (both of which can be found on the app).

Other platforms, like Copper and Greenlight, allow parents to set up chores and pay for them electronically. Linking these apps (and others, like Venmo) through your account will let you instantly transfer those funds into your account.

BEFORE YOU RETIRE. . .

All of the accounts mentioned so far, with the exception of an investment account, earn little to no interest. That's because the reason behind having these accounts is to have money for everyday purchases.

But what if you're thinking long-term?

For starters, congrats. You're not like most teens.

But if long-term savings is your jam, consider opening a retirement account. One of the most popular retirement accounts out there are Roth IRA accounts. There are many awesome (albeit slightly confusing) benefits for starting a Roth IRA, but by far the most important revolves around the concept of compound interest.

Compound interest is the idea that even your interest will add interest.[14]

Wait a second, isn't interest bad? Yes—when it comes to negative interest (like that on a debt or credit card bill), it's bad.

But positive interest is interest that you get to keep. Generally, positive interest is only applied to the principle, or whatever money you have in an account. So, for instance, if you have $100 in an account and earn 2% interest each year, you'll have $102 by the end of the year that you can keep. The next year, you'd have $104. Then $106, and so forth.

But compound interest builds on both the principle and whatever interest is added after the fact. To go back to our previous example, you'd still have $102 after year one but would have $104.04 after year two. And then 106.84. That's because the 2% interest is applied to *everything*.

Okay, a few cents here and there isn't much, I get that. But what if instead of $100, you deposited $1,000? And what if instead of 2% interest, you earned over triple that (most Roth IRAs carry a lifetime interest rate of around 7%)?

Here's what that looks like: if you deposit $1,000 at age 16 and let it sit there, by the time you're 65, that figure will have grown to $22,000. You've done absolutely nothing except let the money grow! Now, if you contribute $500 each year to that account, by the time you're 65, you'll have $187,000 in your Roth account.[15] Now imagine contributing $1,000! $1,500! $2,000!

The bottom line is this: compound interest lets you contribute money to an account now, putting it to work early on. You don't have to be a Wall Street wiz to see your money grow by a factor of 22. You just have to be willing to make a deposit and then forget about it.

THE REAL WORLD ... Here's why it's important to read the fine print when opening any account, especially credit cards: you may miss something. And that "something" could very well cost you thousands of dollars, as it did to the teen we're talking about in this section.[16]

In this case, our teen received one of those exciting letters letting them know that they qualified for a shiny new credit card. This teen filled out the application and waited eagerly for the rectangular piece of plastic to come through the mail.

And when it did, they swiped. And swiped. And swiped.

Until eventually, they crashed hard against the credit card's spending limit. That's right—in a matter of *months*, this card was put through the wringer and maxed out. Even worse—this teen *ignored* messages from the bank that they needed to pay off the card. Not that it would have mattered; the teen made less than $7.00 per hour working around nine hours per week during the school year. At this point, with mounting debt, our teen had to make a hard decision—put the money toward the credit card expenses or spend it on fun outings with friends.

Ultimately, they chose to *not* put the paycheck toward their credit card. The outings continued. The debt stayed. It was a perfect example of *out of sight, out of mind*.

But as we learned in this chapter, those cards earn interest. And for first time users, the interest tends to be much higher than experienced credit card holders. So it didn't take long for the $2,000 in expenses to crawl up to $3,500!

Despite our teen's best wishes, the debt didn't disappear. And it followed them around for years—in job interviews, in apartment lease applications, and car loans.

This story has a happy ending, though. After running out of genie lamps to rub with the hopes of landing three wishes, our teen eventually paid off the debt. *And* they became a finance writer, using their story to empower other teens who might make similar mistakes.

Yes, this teen should have paid off the debt sooner. But not doing so is a common mistake among first-time credit card owners. Fortunately, it wasn't the end of the world. But life gets hard when you don't enter a financial situation prepared and fully knowledgeable.

SUMMARY

It's exciting to see your money grow in an account. It gives you a sense of security. A sense of pride.

But it's hard to keep that money growing without a job. Even if it's a part-time gig, a job will have benefits that go well beyond just adding a little money to your pocket. It could be the difference between getting into a college and hitting the waitlist. It could expose you to fun and exciting careers that you never seriously considered. And, hey, did we mention the employee discounts?

Once you have that job, you'll be ready to open up your first account. But it's not all fun and games; here are a few common mistakes teens make with their first job and accounts:

1. Open the Wrong Account
Research, research, research. If you aren't willing to put in the time beforehand to find the account that's best for you, you run the risk of opening the wrong account based on your individual goals and situation.

It's not an unrecoverable mistake, but why put yourself through the hassle of opening an account only to close it once you realize it's not for you? Do the work on the front end and save yourself some time later.

2. Start Late
Remember the retirement account? You can start putting money into it whenever, but the difference between starting at age 18 and age 28 could be hundreds of thousands of dollars. The same goes for opening an account—you want to start establishing good credit early so that when you're ready to purchase a home or car, you're actually able. Don't worry, we have all of that covered in the next chapter.

3. Don't Read the Fine Print

This is an extension of the first mistake. Once you've made the decision on an account, you must read the fine print so you're completely knowledgeable about what you're getting into. Not reading the fine print is exactly what went wrong with our well-dressed college friend from the example above. Don't be like our friend. Read the fine print. Shop later.

4. Overspend

This is a problem regardless of age or account type. If you spend more money than you make, you'll end up with debt, which can take years to pay off. Even on a smaller scale, a minor overdraft from your checking account will force you to pay $25-$35 in fees, even if you only overspent a dollar or two. A budget helps ensure that you don't overspend and, in the event you do, a budget also helps keep your expenses balanced, including paying off your debts.

5. Find Excuses

This is one for our would-be job seekers who quit the process before finding employment. Whatever the case may be—homework, lack of free time, inexperience—you can always find excuses for not getting a job. But, unless you come into a substantially large amount of money another way, there will come a time when you need to get your first job. Cut out the excuses—if that other kid on your soccer team can balance sports, homework, a job, so can you.

EXERCISE

Hopefully you followed the step-by-step guide on opening a bank account discussed earlier in the chapter. That exercise is arguably the most important of the entire chapter, but as a reminder, we covered more ground than just banking.

Here are a few ideas to get you started on finding that first job. So that you actually have cash to stash in an account.

Build Your Resume

Even if you have zero work experience, chances are you have some life experience that makes you attractive to an employer. Do you play sports? Acted in a school play? Speak multiple languages? Whatever the case, you've gotten to this point by picking up new skills and refining ones that already exist. The hard part isn't figuring out what activities you've done, but rather what skills you've picked up from those activities.

BEGIN BY . . . Make a list of every activity you've been involved in over the last two years. Think about what it took to get there and what you learned as a result of being involved. For example, if you volunteered at a food bank, you probably learned how to communicate effectively in a team environment and also what it means to give back to the community. Communication and selflessness are excellent traits any employer would love to see!

Talk to Your Friends

Stuck with the job search? Ask around to your friends to see what opportunities they've found. Your friends can be an excellent resource when looking for a job because they can explain how they got theirs *and* might even put in a good word for you with the boss.

BEGIN BY . . . There's really only one step to this one: hit up your friends. See what they think about their job!

ENDNOTES

1. Threlkeld, K. (2021, March 11). *Employee Burnout Report: COVID-19's Impact and 3 Strategies to Curb It.* Indeed. https://www.indeed.com/lead/preventing-employee-burnout-report.

2. Cope, D. (2022, February 27). *Experiencing Burnout? Here's how to find your joy at work.* Alabama News Center. https://alabamanewscenter.com/2022/02/27/experiencing-burnout-here-is-how-to-find-your-joy-at-work/.

3. Grove, A. (2020, July 30). *Work Experience and College Applications.* ThoughtCo. https://www.thoughtco.com/work-experience-and-college-applications-4157492#:~:text=Colleges%20value%20work%20experience%20because,students%20who%20don't%20work.

4. Copper (n.d.). *Teen Banking: How to Earn Money as a Teen.* https://www.getcopper.com/guide/earning.

5. Department of Labor (n.d.). *Child Labor—Child Labor Wages.* https://www.worker.gov/child-labor-wages/.

6. Department of Labor. (n.d.). *A Handy Guide to the Fair Labor Standards Act.* https://www.dol.gov/agencies/whd/compliance-assistance/handy-reference-guide-flsa#:~:text=Back%20to%20Top-,Youth%20Minimum%20Wage,of%20employment%20with%20an%20employer.

7. Department of the Treasury. (2022). *Dependants, Standard Deduction, and Filing Information.* https://www.irs.gov/pub/irs-pdf/p501.pdf.

8. Rockwood, K. (2020, September 25). *Banking 101: Understanding How Banks Work.* Step.com. https://step.com/money-101/post/a-teens-guide-to-banking.

9. Wiesniewski, M. (2023, July 06). *What is a Money Market Account.* Bankrate. https://www.bankrate.com/banking/mma/what-is-a-money-market-account/.

10. Johnson, H. (2023, August 30). What is a good APR for credit card? *LA Times.* https://www.latimes.com/compare-deals/credit-cards/guides/good-apr-for-credit-card#:~:text=The%20APR%20you%20receive%20is,APR%20as%20low%20as%2012%25.

11. Fernando, J. (2023, February 09). *Annual Percentage Rate: What it Means and How it Works*. Investopedia. https://www.investopedia.com/terms/a/apr.asp

12. Adams, R. (2023, June 02). *How to Open a Bank Account for a Minor: Steps and What You Need*. Young and the Invested. https://youngandtheinvested.com/how-to-open-a-bank-account-for-a-minor/

13. Egan, J. & Horton, C. (2023, January 24). *Bank Account Minimum Deposit And Minimum Balance Requirements*. Forbes. https://www.forbes.com/advisor/banking/bank-account-minimum-deposit-minimum-balance-requirements/#:~:text=A%20minimum%20opening%20deposit%20is,a%20checking%20or%20savings%20account.

14. Fernando, J. (2023, March 18). *The Power of Compound Interest: Calculations and Examples*. Investopedia. https://www.investopedia.com/terms/c/compoundinterest.asp

15. Bankrate. (n.d.). *Roth IRA Calculator*. https://www.bankrate.com/retirement/roth-ira-plan-calculator/

16. Rox, M. (2015, April 3). *What I did with my first credit card is the perfect example of why teenagers shouldn't have them*. Insider. https://www.businessinsider.com/i-wasnt-ready-for-my-first-credit-card-2015-4

Chapter 5

YOU REALLY ARE JUST A NUMBER, AKA, THE ONE ABOUT CREDIT

A person who pays their bills on time is soon forgotten.
　—Oscar Wilde

It is not the person who has too little, but the person who craves more, that is poor.
　—Seneca

Let's say you hear from Taylor that Charlie has a crush on Sam. But, Taylor also told you that Sam once had a crush on you. And that, as we all remember from *that* viral video that we no longer talk about, was a total lie.

How likely are you to believe Taylor this time?

Probably not much. And for good reason: Taylor led you astray in the past, so you won't be giving them any credit in the future. Heck, Taylor might have to tell you the honest truth 1,000,000 more times in order for you to trust anything they say again.

Turns out you and banks operate in a pretty similar way. If you don't pay your loans on time, then a bank is less likely to believe that you'll pay them on time again in the future. They even assign you a score based on your likelihood of paying back the money that you owe.

This nifty little idea is called credit. And it will, at times, be your best buddy or your mortal enemy.

In this chapter, we're going to demystify credit and show you how important maintaining a strong credit score is to reaching any financial goal you set for yourself. Because just like you might have trouble trusting Taylor again for lying, banks will have a tough time trusting you for missing a loan or debt payment.

THE GHOSTS OF CREDIT'S PAST, PRESENT, AND FUTURE

Remember budgeting? How there were several different definitions depending on the use of the word? Credit is no different.

In one sense, credit refers to a "contractual agreement in which a borrower receives a sum of money or something else of value and commits to repaying the lender at a later date, typically with interest."[1] A loan, for instance, would be an example of credit. You're receiving money that you don't currently have while promising to pay back that money later.

But in other cases (and mostly what we'll discuss in this chapter), credit refers to "the financial soundness of businesses or individuals. Someone who has good or excellent credit is considered less of a risk to lenders than someone with bad or poor credit."[2] Think back to our example to start the chapter: Taylor has bad credit because he's lied in the past. Similarly, someone who's failed to pay back their debts on time has bad credit.

Now, this might not seem fair. *So what, I lied once, and now no one believes me?* Well, yes. Ask the boy who cried wolf how things are going.

But it wasn't always like this. For centuries, buying on credit was reserved for big-time purchases, like a house or farm. But then came the *consumer* credit industry: a fancy phrase that means using credit to make smaller purchases like groceries and clothes.

The idea for the first credit card—the device used to purchase things in the consumer credit industry—came about when a restaurant patron realized he'd left his wallet in another coat. The following year, he returned with a Diners Club card and paid for his meal using the world's first "credit card." After some pitching, he received $1.5 million for his idea for a card that could be used to spend money on various goods and services in New York City. It didn't take long for Visa and Mastercards to jump into the marketplace just two years later.[3]

But as more credit cards began to hit the market, a new need came about. How could people be trusted to pay back whatever they put on a credit card? To solve this problem, various credit bureaus began popping up. Credit bureaus are agencies that keep all of our credit history and create credit reports for banks and lending agencies.

In 1968, TransUnion joined the fray, and in 1996, Experian was founded. A third, the Atlanta-based Equifax, deals primarily in the American southeast. These three credit bureaus are the most trusted in the industry.[4]

UNDERSTANDING YOUR CREDIT

Okay, with that history lesson out of the way, we can get down to brass tacks. First and foremost: your credit report.

Every single person who has ever purchased *anything* on credit has a credit score. These scores range from 300 (bad) to 800 (amazing). These scores are designed to let a credit-lending agency (like a bank) know how likely you are to pay back whatever you owe.[5] This is known as "creditworthiness." If you have a terrible track record of paying off your debts on time, your score will be closer to 300. If you never miss a payment, your score will be closer to 850.

Of course, those aren't the only factors that go into a credit score.[6] Here's the breakdown:

- **Payment History: 35%**
  Are you making payments on time? Failing to make timely payments will ding your score.

- **Amounts Owed:** 30%
  Are you racking up lots of purchases on credit per month? Typically, consistently spending more than 20% of your credit card's limit will ding your score.

- **Length of Credit History:** 15%
  How long have you made purchases using credit? The longer, the better.

- **New Credit:** 10%
  Have you opened any recent credit cards or incurred any debt? Whenever you open a new line of credit, a credit check will occur. Generally, more credit checks ding your score, so it's important to only open a line of credit when you need it.

- **Credit Mix:** 10%
  What types of credit are you opening? The more diverse, the better.

Credit bureaus take all of this information and compile a credit report. That credit report is then used to calculate your credit score. Here's a breakdown of the credit score ranges:[7]

- 300 - 579: Poor (16% of Americans)
- 580 - 669: Fair (18% of Americans)
- 670 - 739: Good (21% of Americans)
- 740 - 799: Very Good (25% of Americans)
- 800 - 850: Exceptional (20% of Americans)

As you might have guessed, you want to be in the "good" range or better, or have a score of 670 or higher.

WHY DO I CARE?

Glad you asked!

It's not fun having your entire financial history boiled down to a single number, but this one number is perhaps the most important to accomplishing your future financial goals.

Chances are, you won't have exactly enough cash on hand to purchase a home. Or your first car. Or maybe you're in a bind and need school textbooks for the first week of September, but won't get paid until the third week of the month.

At any time when you need to make a purchase but don't have cash on hand, you'll need to use credit. And guess where banks go first to determine the parameters of your credit card or loan agreement? Your credit score.

The better your credit history, the better your loan situation will be. You'll qualify for a lower interest rate, better rewards, and a better repayment plan. If you want an apartment, the leasing office will likely perform a credit check to make sure you'll pay your rent on time. Employers might perform credit checks on job seekers along with their background checks. Even your monthly insurance rates are likely to be affected by your credit score.

But even more than that, bad credit history could keep you from getting a loan from a reputable bank, *period*. In that case, you might be tempted to seek out a loan from a sketchy, disreputable company (a "predatory loan company") that could charge upwards of 400% in interest![8] That's an additional $400 on a loan of $100.

Look, most of these consequences are years away for you. Here's why that's great for you: you can start building your credit *now* without feeling weighed down by *needing* to improve your score. That way, by the time your credit score *really matters*, you'll be way ahead of the competition!

HOW TO START

Unfortunately, most banks won't offer credit cards to anyone under 18. But there are still several ways you can start the process of building credit so that when the time comes, you're ready:

- **Get a Job**
  No, a job doesn't help you establish credit. But, it does put money in your account *and* credit scores are affected by income. The higher your income, the better your credit score (generally):

  > *"Your job history, just like your credit history, usually gets stronger with time. The more experience you have, the better your chances of getting a better, higher-paying job in the future, so get started early— without hurting your academics, of course."* [9]

- **Open a Checking and Savings Account**
  Like we discussed in chapter four, put your money to work! Stash your cash! A strong history with a checking and savings account will signal to a bank that you're responsible:

  > *"If you're a responsible account holder with a bank for a while, the bank might be willing to approve you for your first loan or credit card when you're 18."* [10]

- **Become an Authorized User**
  If your parents have credit cards and a positive credit history, see if they'll add you on the card as an authorized user. This means that you can use their credit cards, but you don't have to. In essence, you can reap the rewards without lifting a finger:

  > *"If the adult in question is responsible and pays their bills on time, you can get the benefit of that positive payment history. That's because*

many credit card companies report account details on the credit pro-file of authorized users as well as primary account holders." [11]

Keep in mind that, aside from becoming an authorized user, it will be very hard to start building credit before you turn 18. But these tips are designed to make you as attractive of an applicant as possible when the time does come for you to qualify for a credit card.

But a credit card isn't the only way to build or bust your credit score. It's time for yet another scary four-letter word: loans.

LOANS AND TIGERS AND BEARS, OH MY

You've probably been mis-using the word "borrowing" every day. You ask to "borrow" a sheet of paper in class. You ask to "borrow" a piece of gum. You ask to "borrow" a pencil in class. But how often do you actually return those items?

In fairness, your friend probably doesn't want that gum back.

But you better believe that a bank will want its money back if you borrow from them. Whenever you borrow money from the bank (or anyone, for that matter), you're bringing on debt; the money that you borrow is called a loan.

The person loaning you the money is called the lender (or creditor) while you, the one borrowing the money, are the borrower (or debtor).[12]

Whenever you take out a loan from a bank, you also agree to a re-payment plan. This is a timeline that you promise to pay all the money you borrowed back, plus interest.

INTERESTING

Interest, you say? Back in chapter four, we discussed the idea of compound interest—interest that adds to both the initial deposit (the principle) and any additional interest accrued.

That's the good kind of interest. You get to keep it! But the interest on a loan is the flip side: it's interest that you'll have to pay off, in addition to the initial amount of money that you borrowed. And just as that interest on a Roth IRA adds up quickly, so too does compound interest on a loan that you don't pay off.

Why do we have interest? Because otherwise there'd be no reason for a bank to loan you money. It's how they make money—stashing your money doesn't make them anything and handing out lollipops is a wash. So to make money (and keep their own behinds covered), banks charge interest on a loan. Think of it as the price of them doing you a solid for giving you money when you need it.

And the amount of interest you'll have to pay on the loan (aka the interest rate), is governed in large part by your credit history. Your credit history tells the bank how risky it is for them to lend you money, just like Taylor's history of lying tells you how risky it is for you to trust her.

A bad score means it's a big risk for the bank, because you have a history of not paying back your debts. This will mean a higher interest rate on the loan, because the only way to make the risky loan worthwhile for the bank is if the bank believes it can make more money off the loan.

A good credit score will mean the bank is taking less of a risk with your loan, because you've proven to be trustworthy in paying back what you owe. As a result, you'll get a lower interest rate, which means less you have to pay back.

This is also how credit cards work: they're a loan. The bank is temporarily loaning you the money to pay for new leggings, a concert ticket, or date night at Cold Stone. And the second you make that purchase, you're adding interest.

Let's play a game that hammers the idea of interest on a credit card home. And by game, I mean math puzzle. Buckle up and get out your calculator for this hard-hitting arithmetic lesson.[13]

You go out and buy a pair of Airpods Pro from Amazon, putting it on a credit card. Sick! Those set you back $200, plus an additional $15 in taxes. So, all in, you've put $215 on your credit card.

Let's also say that card charges 20% interest. Use this table to calculate how much those Airpods cost each month that you don't pay them off:

MONTH	AMOUNT	INTEREST	TOTAL OWED
1	$215	20%	(215 x .06) + 215 = 227.90
2	$227.90	20%	
3		20%	
4		20%	
5		20%	

Since the APR (an annualized interest rate) is 20%, you need to divide that by 12 (for months in the year) to calculate the amount of monthly interest you'd pay on the purchase. That comes out to about 0.6%, which is expressed as 0.06 as a decimal. Multiply that figure by the initial payment (215) to get the amount of interest owed on the charge (12.9). Once you add that figure to your initial amount, you get the total amount owed that month: $227.90.

But in this example, you don't pay the card off at the end of the month. This is a) going to hurt your credit score and b) hurt your wallet, because now the same calculation as above must be done again, but instead of 215, you'll have to plug in the new amount of 227.90.

Fill in this chart for the next three months to see how much you'd owe by month five without making a single purchase. Hint: if it doesn't increase each month, you're doing it very, very wrong.

This is why understanding interest and not spending more than you make is so important. Many cards include minimum monthly payments that look enticing, but don't completely eliminate your debt and thus, leave whatever is left to accrue interest.

In the case of big loans (student loans, car loans, mortgage loans, etc.), you'll be required to make monthly loan repayments. These amounts will be fixed ahead of time; for instance, you could be required to pay $350/month on a $30,000 loan until it, and whatever interest the loan has accrued, is paid off.

The time you begin those repayments is also something you and the bank agree to. For big-time payments, the repayment start date could be years down the road. For a credit card, you'll be expected to repay at the end of the month.

AGAIN, WHY DO I CARE?

As a teen, you probably won't have any loans requiring immediate attention. But if you're going to college, you might need to take out a loan to pay for tuition or housing. If you're driving to a job, you might need a loan to pay for a car.

The point is, loans are on the horizon.

And if you aren't paying off your loans or credit card expenses, you could get to the point where all you're doing is paying off the interest, never actually getting to the initial loan or purchase itself. This is how some folks end up paying twice or three times as much as they initially spent, without ever even eliminating any of their debt or buying anything else.

Fortunately, you're probably still in a place where you can *practice* good repayment habits without the pressure of it negatively affecting your credit history. Which is why you'll want to stick around for the exercises portion of this chapter to get that practice in.

THE REAL WORLD . . . For this chapter's real world example, we have a story from someone who began their credit card journey with little financial literacy. What do you notice?

When I went car shopping in my late 20s, I knew my credit was bad. I'd charged up a bunch of credit cards about five years earlier, then let the accounts go to collections because I couldn't pay. But I couldn't bring myself to actually look up my FICO® Score to see just how bad it was.

Delaying the car purchase wasn't an option. My old Corolla had over 200,000 miles on it and was beyond repair, according to my mechanic.

Finally, the guy in the dealership financing office told me the three-digit number I didn't want to know: My FICO® Score was 515. Anything below 579 is generally considered poor -- which means getting credit is hard and you pay exorbitant interest rates when you're approved.

I still drove away in a new (used) Kia Rio that day. It cost $7,700. My only option was to finance it at an atrocious 18% interest rate.

Fortunately, this user was able to crawl out of their bad credit score with time and better habits.

[D]on't be like me. Don't put off looking at your credit reports. Take action before you're in desperate need of financing and have no other choice but to accept terrible terms.[15]

SUMMARY

Credit is often a difficult concept for teens to grasp. Not because it's complicated, not even because the math is tricky, but because so little of it matters right this second. You can begin budgeting now and it'll pay off immediately. You can open a checking account and stash your cash right away.

But before you turn 18, your credit options are limited. Understanding credit, practicing each day, it all comes down to one thing: discipline. Building up good habits now for a future payoff might not be the biggest motivator or resonate the loudest with teens. But here's the deal: your credit *will* matter and it *will* become one of the most important aspects of your financial future.

Take it seriously. And don't make one of these five common credit and loan-related mistakes:

1. Starting Late

You may not be able to build credit right now (unless you become an authorized user), but you can start building good habits. If you have a debit card, don't put yourself into overdraft. Overdrafting on your debit card is like failing to pay back your credit card debt. Keeping your spending in check now will make that process significantly easier down the road.

2. Overuse

Remember that the frequency with which you use a credit card is one of the factors that goes into your credit report. Just because your credit card has a spending limit of $5,000 does not mean you should be putting five grand on it each month.

3. Failure to Understand High-Interest Terms

Make sure you research the terms of any loan agreement or credit card deal. As soon as you sign your name on the dotted line, you're promising to whoever is lending you money that you'll pay them back. Failing to understand the terms or their significance down the line is a major reason why folks struggle to pay off their debts later on. Age and ignorance are no excuses—you'll be legally required to pay whatever you can.

4. Failing to Pay Off Credit Cards Each Month

Many teens see credit cards as "not their money." Which is technically true: whatever money you put on a credit card belongs to a bank. Which means that it might not be your money when you make a purchase, but it will very much be your *problem* when you can't pay the bank back at the end of the month. Get away from this mindset as quickly as possible to avoid falling into this common trap.

5. Not Taking Credit Scores and History Seriously

The benefits to having good credit don't matter on a major level for most teens. You probably won't be taking out a loan to buy a house or a car until you're much older. As a result, teens may not take their credit history seriously as they're making it. Yes, maybe it's a little unfair that decisions you make as a teenager can hurt you into your 30s, but that's just the way the cookie crumbles.

EXERCISE

Here are some easy ways to start building good credit habits now:

Talk to Your Parents About Becoming an Authorized User
Admittedly, this one might take some explaining. But becoming an authorized user is a great way for teens to start building credit before their 18th birthday. You may have to promise not to use the credit card (or only use it on approved purchases), but this exercise is tough to beat.

BEGIN BY. . . Working out an agreement with your parents about what becoming an authorized user would look like. Don't be discouraged if they're hesitant! It's their money that they're letting you potentially in on it.

Develop a "Repayment Plan" with Your Parents
If your parents are skeptical of adding a teenager's name to their account, why not start smaller? See if they'll loan you some money for something you want. A new pair of headphones? Textbooks for school? New cleats for soccer? Anything.

Then, write up a repayment plan (with interest!) that you and your parents agree to follow. If they loan you $100, maybe you agree to pay them the money back with 15% interest. Set monthly payments up (and actually hand the money over, you'll want to simulate actually paying the loan, here) and a target payoff date.

Who knows, once you've proven to be a reliable customer at the BoP (Bank of Parents), they might add you as an authorized user.

EXERCISE (continued)

BEGIN BY. . . Figuring out what you'd like to take a loan out for and what terms you'd feel comfortable agreeing to as a repayment plan. Coming to your parents with a plan will earn you some serious brownie points.

Research Credit Card Options

If you're 16 or 17, you can start researching the right credit card options for you after you turn 18. Cross-compare APRs and rewards. While a starter credit card will likely have few rewards, check out some of the rewards that come with stronger cards. You can earn money back for getting gas, buying groceries, or traveling!

BEGIN BY . . . Using a site like Credit Karma or NerdWallet to compare credit card options based on your financial situation. They'll cue up cards and your likelihood of acceptance based on your credit situation (including none at all!).

ENDNOTES

1. Investopedia. (2023, February 13). *Credit: What It Is and How It Works.* https://www.investopedia.com/terms/c/credit.asp

2. Ibid.

3. Credit Critics. (n.d.). *Ultimate Guide to Understanding Credit for Kids, Teens, and Young Adults.*

4. Investopedia. (2023, February 23). *Top 3 Credit Bureaus: How They Work and What They Know About You.* https://www.investopedia.com/personal-finance/top-three-credit-bureaus/

5. Ibid.

6. Black, M. (2022, September 21). *What Makes Up Your Credit Score.* Forbes. https://www.forbes.com/advisor/credit-score/what-makes-up-your-credit-score/

7. The Ascent. (2021, September 07). *Here's What Americans' FICO® Scores Look Like -- How Do You Compare?* Motley Fool. https://www.fool.com/the-ascent/credit-cards/articles/heres-what-americans-fico-scores-look-like-how-do/

8. Jayakumar, A. & Veling, J. (2023, May 11). *What is Predatory Lending?* NerdWallet. https://www.nerdwallet.com/article/loans/personal-loans/what-is-predatory-lending

9. Acton, B. (2023, March 7). *How to Build Credit Before You Turn 18.* Credit.com. https://www.credit.com/blog/how-high-school-students-can-start-building-credit/#h-why-credit-matters Reprinted with permission.

10. Ibid.

11. Ibid.

12. Family Education. (n.d.). *Teach Kids About Borrowing Money.* https://www.familyeducation.com/teens/values-responsibilities/teach-kids-about-borrowing-money

13. Mountain America Credit Union. (2007). *Teacher's Handbook: Teens and Credit.* https://www.macu.com/media/pdf/teen_lesson_credit.pdf

14. Unasinous. (2014). *Should I get a credit card as a teenager?* Reddit. https://www.reddit.com/r/personalfinance/comments/2d06vs/should_i_get_a_credit_card_as_a_teenager/

15. Hartill, R. (2023, July 19). *4 Things I Wish I Knew When I Had a 515 Credit Score*. Motley Fool. https://www.fool.com/the-ascent/personal-finance/articles/4-things-i-wish-i-knew-when-i-had-a-515-credit-score/ Reprinted with permission.

Chapter 6

WAIT, I CAN INVEST??

If you're prepared to invest in a company, then you ought to be able to explain why in simple language that a fifth grader could understand, and quickly enough so the fifth grader won't get bored.
　—Peter Lynch

Dogs have no money. Isn't that amazing? They're broke their entire lives. But they get through.
　—Jerry Seinfeld

So you finally got that job at the ice cream shop. Sick! You'll be spending more time shoveling Moose Tracks into cups and cones and less time in your own mouth (trust me, your wallet will be happy for this).

Everything is awesome about the job, except for *that one person*. You know who I'm talking about; they exist in every single group setting. The one who works a bit harder than you, who makes things look easy, who, no matter what you do, always comes out a bit ahead.

What they're probably doing is working *smarter*, not harder.

When it comes to personal finance, one of the biggest ways to work smarter is by letting your money do the work *for you*. How cool would that be? Well, it's possible. It even has a name: investing.

THE WOLF OF MAIN STREET

When you hear the word "investing," what comes to mind? Wall Street? Suspenders? Bulls? Bears? Weird three and four-letter abbreviations that scroll across a ticker screen alongside red and green numbers?

What you're thinking of is the stock market, which is a form of investment. But at its base, investing is all about actions you take with your money to make it grow.[1] The idea is that if you put in a little money now, you'll earn more sometime in the future. It's like gardening—planting a small seed now could yield a massive redwood!

Or if gardening isn't your thing, think of it like any sport. You might pay for soccer lessons with the hope that you'll make the varsity team down the line. That initial payment for lessons is an investment in your sports future.

Financial investments work like this: You give someone (or something) money in exchange for a stake in whatever it is that they're doing. The idea is that once that "thing" grows in value, your own stake will have grown as well.

Here's an example. In 1976, Apple was worth roughly $8,000. That means $800 would have bought you around 10% of the company's overall stake. Nearly 50 years and a few iPhones later, Apple is valued in the *trillions* of dollars. As a result, that $800 in 1976 would have grown to (roughly) $280 billion in 2022.[2] That's how much Ronald Wayne, who owned 10% of Apple in 1976, would have today had he not sold his shares for $800 at the time. Ouch.

While you might not make billions of dollars, you get the idea. Investing is a key way to add to your wealth outside of a traditional job. This is only fair—if you have to work, so should your money!

Lucky for you, teens can invest in things as well. In fact, your age might be your biggest advantage in the entire investing game.

"Age is arguably a younger investor's most valuable asset. This is because of compound interest, or the ability of your money to start earning its own money," says Taylor Jessee, a CPA and CFP and the director of financial planning for financial consulting firm Taylor Hoffman. "The earlier you start investing, the longer you'll have your money being put to work for you."[3]

As the Apple example tells us, you don't even need tons of money in order to invest. But what you will need is, and say it with me now, *a rich uncle*. Just kidding, it's a plan. You need a plan.

CHART THE COURSE

There are three components to an investment plan that you'll need to work out: 1) Your Style, 2) Your Budget, and 3) Your Risk Tolerance. Let's break them down.

1) Your style

What do the Met Gala, investing, and figure skating have in common? In order to succeed at each, you need a distinct style.

Here's the key question for understanding your investment style: *How much time am I willing to put into investing my money?* There are two camps on this one: active investing and passive investing.[4] Here are the key differences:

ACTIVE INVESTING	PASSIVE INVESTING
Actively participating in the day-to-day operations of investment, usually through an online brokerage.	Putting your work into investment vehicles while someone else maintains the account.

In other words, active investing involves more work, more risk, and more potential reward, while passive investing revolves around more simplicity, more stability, and more predictability.

Think about your own situation, now. Are you in a place where you can dedicate significant time to investing? Do you know how to research? Do you have the funds to pay someone else to invest your money for you?

If you're willing to put the time into not just following investment trends but also doing the research, active investing might be for you. But if you have the money to let someone else make smart decisions while you buff up on your finance knowledge, then passive investing could be the move.

2) Your budget

In order to determine your style, you'll also need to determine your budget. Ask yourself how much money you have to invest, and go from there.

Keep in mind there's no wrong answer when starting out. As a teen, you might already feel your money pulled in various directions—entertainment, gas, clothes—but setting aside even a few dollars every month could be the difference in, well, billions, as our Apple example teaches.

Also, don't throw out the rulebook on the budgeting chapter. You still need an emergency fund, you still need to set aside money for mandatory expenses, and you still need to spend less than you make. But think of investments as a cherry on top of your budget—it'll make the whole thing a little sweeter.

3) Your risk tolerance

For the entirety of your investing career, risk tolerance will be a phrase you come to know well. This factor is all about how much risk you're willing to run with your investments. That's because not every investment is created equally. Some are safe, with almost guaranteed levels of return. Others are extremely risky, a boom-or-bust gamble that could backfire just as easily as it could pay off.

Think about it: the Apple investment looks like a no-brainer now, but in 1976, it was so risky that someone wasn't willing to keep $800 locked into it. In 1976, no one was sure if Apple's value would increase or if the company would fold.

As an adult, you may have significant financial obligations, like a house payment or a child. As a result, you might only want to put your money in safer, proven investments. Chances are, though, that those safer investments won't yield the same returns as a boom-or-bust investment.

But as a teen, you might be able to take on a little more risk. For one, your financial obligations are likely very low. In addition, you have a greater amount of time to lose an investment and recover from them.

Generally, though, it's always nice to have a mix. Balance is everything. So, when you begin to create your portfolio (a fancy term for your collection of investments), be sure to put your money into a combination of risky bets and safe bets. That way, even if your risk doesn't pay off, you aren't completely out of luck.

Now, you may be wondering what risky and safe investments actually look like. Don't worry—you'll learn all about specific investments in chapter seven.

For now, we'll focus on ways to actually make investments as a teenager by using a nifty set-up called a brokerage account.

BROKERAGE > GOING BROKE

Bad news: Most investments require you to be 18 years or older in order to participate. The good news: You and your parents or guardian can open up a custodial brokerage account.

Let's back up for a minute. A brokerage account is an account that lets you make investments. You can see your entire portfolio in one place and adjust it as needed. For that, you'll need 18 candles on the birthday cake.

However, a custodial brokerage account gives a minor ownership of the assets in the account but allows the adult on the account to make investment and withdrawal decisions. Then, once the minor turns 18 (or, in some states, 21), full possession of the account shifts to them.[5]

There is another option: a guardian account. These are reserved for special circumstances, though, and usually mandated by the court.

Guardian accounts are usually set up when a minor or adult cannot handle their finances properly due to mental or physical incapacitation. These are also known as "conservatorships." Famously, Britney Spears was locked into this type of account until she successfully sued in 2021 and had her conservatorship removed.[6]

Finally, there are special accounts, like the Roth IRA account, discussed several chapters back. When you deposit money into a Roth account, you're making an investment; generally, a Roth is made up of stocks, bonds, and mutual funds (don't worry — that's coming next chapter). For now, just understand that the way Roth IRA accounts (and any other specialized retirement account) make money is through investments in the market.

Here's a list of several account options and what situations they're best for[7]:

ACCOUNT TYPE	BEST FOR...
Custodial Brokerage Account	*If a teen doesn't have taxable income or wages; teaching about smart investing*
Roth IRA	*If a teen does have taxable income or wages*
ABLE Account (Guardian Account)	*If a teen has a disability*
529 Plan	*If saving for a teen's education is the desired outcome*

To get you started with day-to-day investing, a custodial brokerage account is the way to go. It offers a low-risk opportunity to learn the ins and outs of investing. A Roth, for instance, is designed to put money in it and leave it alone. A custodial brokerage, though, gives you a bit more flexibility to play with; it's not exclusively designed for the long haul.

And did we mention, that you *and* your parents can invest *together* with a custodial brokerage account, and what teen doesn't love bonding time with the folks who birthed them?

Here's how to get started setting up a custodial brokerage account:

START IT UP

The first step in the process of opening up a custodial account is making sure that's the right account for you. If learning the basics of investing is your goal, then you're in the right place. But if that's *not* the preferred outcome, consult the last table and make your decision.

Next, and at the risk of being a bit too obvious here, open the account. Using a broker, the process can be done in 15 minutes or less, provided you have all of the right documentation. As for a broker, some of the most common are H&R Block, Fidelity, and.

You'll need Social Security Numbers for both a parent and teen, as well as dates of birth and contact information to successfully open the account. Also, be ready to link the account to a bank so that you can start funding the custodial account.

Finally, it's time to have some fun. Parents and teens should work together to come up with a list of possible stocks to invest in. Check out the stock's history, returns, annual reports, and any current events related to the company that might affect the stock's price. For instance, if the government announces a major initiative to invest in solar panels, a solar panel manufacturer might be an excellent investment!

Narrow that list to one or two individual stocks, for now. Put a little money into it and watch it grow! Or, if the stock doesn't do so hot, watch it fall. Discuss why that happened and how you use that lesson to make a better decision next time around.

Also, it might help to keep that account diversified, especially if you're consistently adding money to it. Research a few ETFs and mutual funds to add to your portfolio (these will be explained in greater detail next chapter).

OTHER OPTIONS

Wouldn't it be nice if there was a way to actually practice investing without running the risk of losing any money? Turns out—there is!

Most brokerage firms offer programs called "paper trading," which simulate the experience of investing without money. The term comes from an old practice with young traders, where they'd actually handwrite and invest on paper, calculating their wins and losses, before actually going forward with any trading.

Paper trading simulates real investing in the stock market *without* using any real money. You can start out with however much "paper money" (i.e. fake money) you want to invest and divide your budget up accordingly. But don't expect any huge returns—any returns you have paper trading are as useful as Monopoly money.

Take this process seriously: you'll not only learn the ins and outs of investing in the market, but also understand what it takes to be an active investor (if that's your style).

The recommendation is to paper trade for at least six months before investing with real money. That way, you'll have plenty of experience both seeing your money grow and, very likely, seeing more than a few of your stocks fail to work out.

At the end of that six months, evaluate how you've done. Did you make as much money as you hoped? Which stocks didn't pan out, and why? Alternatively, which stocks *did* pan out, and why? After those six months, you'll start noticing patterns that will help you when it comes to laying down more than just monopoly money.

THE REAL WORLD . . . Teens around the world are using the power of investments to their advantage. But with all things, it takes a thorough understanding of your style, budget, and risk tolerance in order to see a return on your investment.

And, as is the case with our real-world example, Brandon Fleisher, a little help from your parents never hurts. Brandon's story, which has been covered by multiple outlets, including CNN, is one not only of smart investing, but also of paying the knowledge forward.

It all started when Brandon's 8th grade math teacher instructed the class to follow a single stock, tracking its peaks and valleys. Most teens might pick a familiar name—Apple, Spotify—but not Brandon. In lieu of a well-known name, Brandon selected Avalon Rare Metals, which happened to go gangbusters by the end of the experiment.

Brandon continued following stocks, even after the end of his 8th grade experiment. Eventually, he got so good at paper trading, his parents co-signed a direct account and gave him $48,000 to invest. Brandon wasn't just dealing with monopoly money anymore; it was his parents' savings.

Here's how Brandon does it: he's an active investor. More than that, he's attracted to smaller companies that "make their leadership accessible," thereby giving the investors a behind-the-scenes look at the company's inner workings.[8]

Now, Brandon is working to spread the word. He owns a financial newsletter—The Financial Bulls—and oversees a team of writers who deliver investing advice to folks of all ages, but is primarily written by younger investors.

From this real-world profile, we know several things: Brandon is someone who is an active investor (he's in the weeds, constantly reviewing the companies he wishes to invest in).

His budget was $48,000, a hefty sum that he only landed after proving to his parents that he would be responsible with their money.

As for his risk tolerance? He's willing to risk a bit more on companies that he's done research into, rather than longer-term guarantees. Brandon exemplifies all of the steps discussed in this chapter!

SUMMARY

Between this chapter and the next, this one is easily the less glamorous. You'll learn about stocks and ETFs and mutual funds and all of the specifics behind *what* to invest in next. But without the lessons in this chapter, you'd be lost at sea trying to invest.

That's because this chapter has been all about making a plan, which really epitomizes the entire purpose of personal finance. You're planning for your future and getting practice in today.

But investing is one area where you can go even further than just practice. Paper trading might be a no-risk simulator, but a brokerage account is a very real account involving very real money.

Once you understand your style, your budget, and risk tolerance, you're ready to hit the ground running. But without it, without a *plan*, you risk falling flat on your face.

COMMON MISTAKES

1. Being Unprepared

There's no way around it: you have to do your planning. And you have to take that planning *seriously*. Spend time to figure out your style, your budget, and risk tolerance ahead of time. Otherwise, you'll find yourself scrambling down the line after you've invested your money. Doing your research ensures that your goals align with your reality.

2. Burning Out/Quitting Too Soon

Remember our friend Ronald Wayne? The one who sold his shares of Apple a few decades too early? It's easy to lose faith in investing or get scared off by negative headwinds. But here's the deal: that stock *did* rise, but it took 50 years to see its valuation hit the billions of dollars. Investing takes patience, which can be derailed if you go all in too quickly, only to lose interest before you really start to see your money grow.

Pace yourself and give yourself time to get this right. If it doesn't work out your first time, that's okay! Remember that you're still a teen—you can take mistakes in the present. Your biggest advantage is time; don't squander it because of a few temporary setbacks.

3. Setting the Wrong Budget

It's hard saving a few dollars here and there, especially as a teen. Why invest for the long haul when you can use that money for immediate satisfaction? After all, the stock market will always be there, but BTS only comes to town once.

This all goes back to budgeting. If you're honest and disciplined with your budgeting, you'll discover ways to set aside a few bucks every month that you can dedicate to investing. If you set aside $20 each month, you'll have nearly $250 by the end of the year. That's more than enough to kickstart your investing journey.

(continued) SUMMARY

4. Starting Late

Remember, the entire purpose of investing as a teen is to get a head start on the competition. The earlier you start, the longer you have to a) make money and (perhaps more importantly) b) learn from your mistakes.

5. Taking It Unseriously

Commitment is everything when it comes to investing. You've probably heard the saying "You get out what you put in" before, and it's true here. The worst thing you can do is take this process with a lax attitude; remember: it's your money! Because teens rely on their parents to fulfill most of their needs, many don't properly understand the value of the dollar. That's not necessarily a teen's fault, it's only natural.

That said, failing to take this process seriously only delays learning the value of money. Further, you're not *really* learning anything if you invest willy-nilly. Maybe it works every once in awhile, but few people grow their money with only a blasé attitude.

EXERCISE

Try out these exercises to get you started on your investing journey:

Research a Few Stocks of Interest

Before you take any test, you have to do your homework. Or before any big game, you have to get reps in at practice. Before the band concert, how many times do you play the piece? Probably enough to do it in your sleep.

Investing involves the same process. Do your homework on available investments and which might provide for some nice returns.

BEGIN BY. . . Finding five stocks that you would feel comfortable investing your money into. In addition, write out a list of pros and cons for investing in the stock and the reasoning behind why you wish to invest in these specific stocks over others.

Play Around with Paper Trading Sites

Once you have those five stocks in mind, it's time (fake) invest! Set up an account on a paper trading website, set your budget, and get to work! Be realistic about your budget too—you may feel tempted to start with a budget of $1,000,000, but chances are you won't have quite that much to actually invest in.

BEGIN BY. . . Setting up your paper trading account. WeBull, Schwab, and Tradovate are excellent options.

ENDNOTES

1. Easy Peasy Finance. (n.d.). *What is Investing? A Simple Explanation for Kids, Teens & Beginners.* https://www.easypeasyfinance.com/investing-for-kids-financial-literacy/

2. Bry, A. (2022, April 12). *This Apple Cofounder Sold His Stake For $800 On This Day In 1976: How Much Would It Be Worth Now?* Bezinga. https://www.bezinga.com/tech/22/04/26589263/this-apple-cofounder-sold-his-stake-for-800-on-this-day-in-1976-how-much-would-it-be-worth-now

3. Gobler, E. (2022, June 20). *Investing for Teens: Everything You Need to Know.* The Balance Money. https://www.thebalancemoney.com/investing-guide-for-teens-and-parents-4588018

4. Frankel, M. (2023, July 07). *How to Invest Money: Getting Started with Investing.* Motley Fool. https://www.fool.com/investing/how-to-invest/

5. Beers, B. (2023, March 24). *How to Open a Brokerage Account for a Child.* Investopedia. https://www.investopedia.com/ask/answers/can-someone-not-yet-legal-age-open-brokerage-account/

6. Farrow, R. & Tolentino, J. (2021, July 03). Britney Spears's Conservatorship Nightmare. *New Yorker.* https://www.newyorker.com/news/american-chronicles/britney-spears-conservatorship-nightmare

7. Durana, A. & O'Sheana, A. (2023, June 02). *Investing for Kids: How to Open a Brokerage Account for Your Child.* NerdWallet. https://www.nerdwallet.com/article/investing/set-kids-brokerage-account

8. Gillespie, P. (2015, April 28). *Meet the 17-year-old investor who tripled his money.* CNN. https://money.cnn.com/2015/04/28/investing/millennial-investor-17-year-old-brandon-fleisher/

Chapter 7

SHUT UP AND TAKE MY MONEY

It's not how much money you make, but how much money you keep, how hard it works for you, and how many generations you keep it for.
—Robert Kiyosaki

I know many people who have a lot of money, and they get testimonial dinners, and they get hospital wings named after them. But the truth is that nobody in the world loves them. That's the ultimate test of how you have lived your life. The trouble with love is that you can't buy it.... But the only way to get love is to be lovable. It's very irritating if you have a lot of money. You'd like to think you could write a check: I'll buy a million dollars worth of love. But it doesn't work that way. The more you give love away, the more you get.
—Warren Buffett[1]

Way back in Chapter 6, you learned that there are plenty of ways for young people to begin their investing journey before they hit 18. But knowing you can invest is only half the battle—it's like knowing you can drive a car without having four wheels to practice.

In this chapter, we're going to dive into the various ways you can put your money to work and how to select the investment option that makes the most sense for you.

Let's start with probably the most common and familiar form of investing: stocks and bonds.

BONDS. STOCKS AND BONDS.

It's time to talk about the stock market. A stock is a share of a company; when you purchase a stock, you're actually purchasing a sliver of that company and becoming a shareholder. The more stock you own, the more decision-making authority you have in the company.

When you buy a company's stock, you're taking a bet on the company's future. If you purchase some stock now, the price will increase over time so that you can sell it for a profit down the road.

For instance, let's say Apple's stock is going for around $145 per share (this is where it was in January 2023). That means owning a piece of Apple will cost you $145. You can buy up as much stock as you want, so long as you have the money to pay for it. Maybe you've worked a few extra shifts and have enough money to buy three shares, which would cost $435 total.

Now, you can hang onto that stock and watch your money grow. You wait and wait until you decide it's the perfect time to cash out, ideally when the stock has increased in value. Apple's stock topped out at $196 in July 2023. So, if you sold it for that price, you'd receive $588, over $153 in profit!

Of course, it's not always this magical. Let's say the reverse happened—you purchased the stock for $196 per share, but it dropped to $145. In that case, you'd be out $153 because the value of the stock decreased.

This is why the stock market can be such a risk. There are many stocks—like Apple, Google, Amazon, etc.—that are likely safe bets to increase over time. But others, like newer companies or ones undergoing any sort of leadership change or auditing, can sink like a rock.

You can gain access to investing in stocks through a number of services, including Charles Schwab. Fidelity even has a few stock "Youth Accounts" designed to get teens interested in investing.[2]

When selecting the stocks to invest in, it's important to remember your risk tolerance, which we covered in the last chapter. As a teen, you may feel like your risk tolerance is a bit higher since you're a bit insulated from the pressures of bills and major expenses. Or maybe you want low-risk options that may pay off longer in the super long-run, which is a major boost for you since you're starting out so early. Either way, it's important to make sure that your investment goals line up with your ability to withstand and tolerate risk.

Bonds, on the other hand, are essentially the super low-risk alternative to stocks. The key difference is buying a bond is loaning money to a company, not owning a company. In most cases, the bond is set for a specific term (or amount of time). The end of the term is known as the date that the bond matures.

In a sense, you get to be the banker for the company (or even government) that you loan money to. That means the money you loan to the bank (i.e. the bond) earns interest over time. In addition, when the bond matures, you get your initial loan back.

These tend to be popular holiday gifts from (especially older) relatives that are supposed to be a bit safer than giving a kid cold hard cash. In some families, it's tradition to take out a bond for a newborn and let it earn interest over the course of their childhood (or life) so that when they become adults, they get a nice little payday.

One of the most common forms of bonds are government bonds. And because the government is considered extremely reliable when it comes to paying back what it owes, the bonds tend to be safe bets. The counter is that the rate of return on a bond tends to be lower than what you might make in the stock market.

Again, it all comes down to your investment profile and risk assessment.

MUTUAL FUNDS

Geesh, there are so many stocks and bond options to choose from. How do you go about sorting them all? How do you sift through the studs from the duds?

Maybe that's not quite your jam. Instead, investment companies offer mutual funds to cut through the hassle of picking individual stocks. These are collections of stocks and bonds that are bundled together and invested in at one time by a fund manager. You make money like you would through any ordinary stock or bond, but the risk is often less because you're investing in a diverse companies.

Think of the stock market as a big buffet. It can be challenging to pick the right combination of foods (and, by extension, make the healthy options). Picking out stocks and bonds on your own is like going through the buffet line yourself—you might get close to a balanced meal, or you might pick up two slices of chocolate cake that taste way better going down than they do sitting in your belly.

A mutual fund is basically like having a nutritionist go through the buffet line for you. They know how to properly select the food that will make you feel the best; instead of two slices of chocolate cake, the mutual fund manager will make sure you get your cake (and broccoli and pasta and protein) *and* eat it too.

EXCHANGE-TRADED FUNDS

Similar to a mutual fund, an exchange traded fund (ETF) is a collection of stocks that take the headache and guesswork out of investing.

The key difference is that ETFs are offered by the stock market itself, rather than pulled together by a fund manager. This means that when you invest in an ETF, you aren't *exactly* investing in the companies represented by the ETF. Instead, you're investing in a fund that aims to track the strength and wellbeing of the collection of stocks it represents. While mutual funds are only traded once per day, ETFs are constantly traded and subject to daily fluctuation.

That said, these tend to be excellent, low-cost options for baby investors. Because you don't have to hire someone to do the investing for you, you save plenty of money along the way.

CERTIFICATES OF DEPOSIT (CDs)

Don't worry, we won't make any "CDs are so '90s" jokes in this section.

Certificates of Deposit are similar to bonds in that they are a loan that earns interest over time. The only difference is that CDs are made to banks, meaning you get to loan the bank money and have it earn interest over time, generally a period agreed to by the bank and customer. My how the tables have turned!

CDs are extremely low-risk, since banks are insured up to $250,000 by the FDIC. So even if your bank suddenly collapsed (unlikely) before you cashed in your CD, you'd still be covered.

The downside? The interest paid out is generally extremely low. The longer you go, though, the higher the interest rate. But don't expect to make it rich off of a CD. At the end of the agreed-upon time, you'll get your initial principal(investment) back.

RETIREMENT PLANS

We've touched on this concept already, but as a reminder: retirement accounts are excellent ways to put money away for the future and have it grow without you thinking about it. Roth IRAs are a popular option, since the interest is compounded over time, which means high growth rates in the long, long run.

In addition to a Roth IRA, your employer might fund a 401(k). A 401(k) plan works similar to a Roth, but you elect how much of your paycheck you'd like to contribute to the plan. Your employer then sets aside the designated amount (usually capped out at a few thousand dollars per year), so you don't have to do anything!

The great part about retirement accounts is that you can put your pretax earnings in them and then take them out without paying taxes on them, assuming you have held the money in the account for a minimum of five years. Again, there are some limits to what you can contribute, but the tax advantages are strong.

OPTIONS

Options are like stocks with a twist. Instead of buying a stock, you're paying for a contract to buy or sell a stock at a given price at a given time. Essentially, you haven't bought or sold the stock yet, but have the *option* to at a certain date if the price is right.

If your option works out, you can make a ton of money by buying a stock at a lower price and then selling high. But if it doesn't work out, you've only committed to the price of the contract, so the losses aren't as significant.

> WORD OF WARNING: *options are a fairly complex investment and probably not suited for teens just starting out in their investing journey. Leave this one up to the Wall Street experts.*

ANNUITIES

Think of an annuity as a supplement to your retirement plan. You purchase the annuity (generally an insurance policy) that then pays you down the road. Most annuities are purchased at a given date but not actually paid out until retirement.

But, like CDs, annuities aren't super high growers. Rather, they're often used as a separate income stream once you've hit your golden years.

COMMODITIES

So far, we've talked about investing in non-tangible things—stocks, insurance policies, retirement accounts, etc. These are things that you can't actually hold; they're made-up concepts we all just sort of agree to.

But commodities are different. Commodities are real things—gold, oil, real estate—that you can invest in. But keep in mind, as a teen investor, commodities are often closely linked to current events. For instance, an oil spill in the Gulf of Mexico could see oil commodity investments plummet. As a result, they tend to be a bit riskier than other investments and are, like options, usually best reserved for folks with a bit more experience.

REAL ESTATE AND PROPERTY INVESTMENTS

One of the most popular commodity investments is real estate. According to one investing expert, real estate is one of the safest bets on the investing circuit: *Real estate investing is safe and secured by the asset itself—the building. Rarely will you see your investment lose value and if so, it's usually only for a short period of time. Unlike fiat currencies like the dollar, real estate doesn't lose value to inflation year after year—it performs better.*[3]

But as a teen, are you really ready to just start dropping wads of cash on houses, buildings, and plots of land? The answer is a bit more complex than you might think.

Before diving into how teens can get involved in investing in real estate, let's go over a few common forms of real estate investing, along with pros and cons behind each.[4] Ultimately, this will help set the stage for picking which investment is right for you.

Residential real estate

This is probably the most commonly-thought of form of real estate investments. Residential real estate is real estate designed for people to live in—it's their "residence."

Here are a few common examples of residential real estate properties:

1. **Long-Term Rental Property:** A property you own with the intention of renting out for an extended period of time. You make money by charging a rent to the tenants living in the property.

2. **Vacation Rental:** a property you own, typically in an area popular with tourists (like a beach), and rent out for short periods of time. You make money by charging people to stay on the property.

3. **Flipping Houses:** This is the HGTV route of real estate investing. When you flip a home, you purchase a fixer-upper and put the necessary time and money into improving the home to then sell it for more money on the back-end. It requires a bit of cash to start out, between purchasing the home and buying the equipment for repairs.

4. **Micro-Flipping:** If home improvement isn't your specialty, you might try micro-flipping, which is the process of buying an undervalued home and then reselling it quickly, ideally for more money. You make fewer repairs and spend less money, but also make less than you would flipping houses.

5. **Accessory Dwelling Units (ADUs):** A part of your property that serves as a living space (like a basement) and is rented out, typically to a family member.

PROS OF RESIDENTIAL REAL ESTATE	CONS OF RESIDENTIAL REAL ESTATE
If you're willing to work hard and know what you're doing, you can make significant returns on your initial investment.	Real estate investing is time consuming. You're responsible for any repairs needed, which can also get expensive, especially when flipping houses.
Real estate appreciates in value, so there's a good chance that if you sell your residential property in the future, you'll make money on your investment.	You often have to wait for your real estate investment to truly appreciate in value. Aside from micro-flipping, you may have to wait to see your investment grow.
You receive tax deductions on residential real estate property you own.	You need a decent nest egg of funds when starting out; it's nearly impossible to invest in real estate without a fairly sizeable initial investment.

Commercial real estate

Unlike residential real estate, commercial real estate is about investing in places where people work—where "commerce" is conducted. Hotels, warehouses, and business parks are all common examples of commercial real estate. Next time you go to a big city, look for skyscrapers with company names on them (like 30 Rock in New York)—those are commercial (and probably house more than just one company).

But like residential real estate, you make money by charging the tenants a rent to use the space. Usually, the rental agreement stipulates that the space is to be used only for commercial purposes. You can also sell the property itself in the future once it appreciates in value.

PROS OF COMMERCIAL REAL ESTATE	CONS OF COMMERCIAL REAL ESTATE
Commercial real estate nets a higher return on your investment than residential real estate, since you're charging rent to businesses instead of people.	Because you're renting to businesses, your risk inherently goes up. While a residential property owner might just worry about property damage, a commercial owner should familiarize themselves with local personal injury and premises liability laws.
The value of commercial real estate is dictated by how much revenue it brings in. As a result, if the business renting is successful, you might be able to sell the property quicker and for more money than a residential property.	You may juggle multiple tenants at one time, which can become tricky and confusing.
There is often a more professional relationship between the tenant and owner in a commercial real estate agreement than residential. As a result, the upkeep required in a commercial property versus residential may be less risky.	While it might be less risky, you probably need to hire out a professional cleaning and maintenance staff to keep the place tidy.

Raw land

Raw land is exactly what it sounds like: land without anything on it. No buildings, roads, or any other development to speak of. Essentially, investing in raw land is investing in the property for what it *could* become.

In many cases, landowners lease the land they own to farmers or seek out property development companies to build on the land and sell it for an appreciated value in the future. Other times, folks will take out land loans on raw land that they intend to build on (and use whatever revenue from the land development to pay back the loan).

PROS OF RAW LAND	CONS OF RAW LAND
Raw land tends to be easier to acquire and costs less money upfront than other developed properties.	Raw land has far fewer tax advantages than developed property.
Since there's nothing there, there's little on your end that requires maintenance.	While the investment in raw land is likely to appreciate in value, it might take longer than developed property to do so.
The options are endless with raw land. You can buy it, sell it, develop it, leave it alone. Whatever you want, you can make it happen.	While you have more options with raw land, you do need to be wary of zoning laws. Local governments regulate what type of buildings can be constructed and maintained in a given part of town. For instance, you may not be allowed to build a warehouse in a section of town that's zoned for residential housing. Even then, you might face challenges from a city government in getting approval to build on an empty lot.

Real estate investment trusts (REITs)

If the day-to-day operation of a real estate property between soccer practice and homework doesn't exactly sound thrilling, that's okay. You may wish to invest in REITs, which are companies that oversee several real estate investments. Instead of outright owning a property, you can invest in the REIT and receive income for revenue generated by the REIT. A number of REITs are publicly traded on the stock exchange, including Tanger Outlets (shopping) and Diversified Healthcare Trust (hospitals/medical parks).[5]

PROS OF REITS	CONS OF REITS
The workload involved with a REIT is minimal—all you have to do is invest the money and let the REIT handle the rest.	REITs are taxed at a higher rate than traditional stocks.
Depending on the REIT, the income tends to be fairly steady.	Though steady, the income might not be significant in the short term.
Though many REITs are stocks, they keep your portfolio of investments diversified since this is a real estate-based investment.	The lack of workload also means a complete lack of control over the properties themselves.

Real estate crowdfunding

Thanks to technology, finding a group of investors has never been easier. That's especially true with real estate crowdfunding, a form of investment that involves investors pooling their money to go in on something they wouldn't otherwise be able to purchase on their own.

Platforms like CrowdStreet offer an easy way for investors to find one another, but many require a minimum income threshold to participate.[6]

PROS OF CROWDFUNDING	CONS OF CROWDFUNDING
Affords investors unique opportunities that otherwise wouldn't exist without the technology.	Any dividends you receive from crowdfunding is taxed.
Very little effort required, with the entire process usually completed virtually.	The minimum income threshold prevents certain groups of people from participating.
Excellent opportunity to diversify an investment portfolio.	The crowdfunding platforms likely will charge a user fee, which adds to the expenses of investment.

HOW TO GET STARTED

Here's the deal with any of these real estate investments: it probably costs a pretty penny to even *start*. Even raw land can cost *millions* of dollars depending on the location.

In other words, you'd probably have to pick up quite a few extra shifts at work in order to save up even a fraction of enough to buy that vacant lot next to the highway that you're sure has oil underneath. Not to mention the fact that you can't exactly take calls from needy tenants in the middle of a pop quiz on Macbeth. Hamlet, *maybe*. But certainly not Macbeth.

That said, there are still plenty of ways you can get involved in real estate, if that's the path you wish to follow.[7] It's a smart move—real estate almost always appreciates in value, and finding a way in at age 16 could see serious rewards by the time you're 26.

Here are six strategies to getting a start in real estate, even as a teenager:

1. **Educate yourself.** Ugh, more homework? On the plus side, at least you're an expert in studying. Or should be, anyway. Before putting any money down for property, you need to familiarize yourself with the area itself. Read books, listen to podcasts, watch YouTube videos— any way that you can develop a foundation in understanding the ins and outs of real estate will help you make the investment decision possible when the time comes.

2. **Have a business plan.** To get from soccer practice in one part of town to math tutoring in another, you probably need a map. Business works the same way—you need a plan. Figure out what your individual goals are, what your company's mission and values will be, and how you plan to get to the finish line. This plan will serve as your compass when faced with a challenging decision— stick to it, and you'll set yourself up well.

3. **Get a real estate mentor.** Here's a little secret about adults: they love to help young people coming up in their profession. Seriously. They *love* it. Don't be afraid to reach out to someone who's blazed a similar trail to you. Services like LinkedIn make it easy to find potential mentors to reach out to and get advice from. They can advise you on mistakes they made and what they'd do differently based on their own experiences.

4. **Exercise financial discipline.** Remember, real estate investing is pricey. If you're serious about getting started, you'll need a large initial investment, which requires saving money. And once you're

making money, stay diligent about your spending and speak with a financial advisor (most likely the parental units) who can help create a savings plan to reach your goals.

5. **Establish your credit.** Chances are you'll find yourself hoping to take out a property or land loan to finance a real estate project. And in order to get the best loan possible with the lowest interest rates, you'll need a strong credit history. Get started today, and brush up on our lesson from Chapter 5.

6. **Partner up.** Isn't it nice splitting the bill at dinner? Real estate works the same way: find someone you trust and don't mind working with to help offset the workload and cost of investing in real estate. Seriously, though, make sure it's someone you trust. Your best friend, love them to death, may not be the right choice if they're not perfectly aligned with your goals and financial discipline.

As a teenager, you may not have the time or money to fully dedicate yourself to investing in real estate. The point here is to develop a foundation so that when you *do* have that time and money, you're ready to go for it. For now, stick with smaller-scale investment opportunities.

Maybe you think investing in real estate is a bit of leap, like going from JV football to the NFL. And in truth, it's not the easiest investment avenue for teens. That said, it's not impossible.

For instance, two teens in my town decided to go the real estate route. They had a bold idea: work full-time at Walgreens while also attending high school. After six months, they took all of their earnings and invested it into a rental property. A few months later, and they had made enough money to invest in *another* rental.

How'd they do it? For starters, their expenses were small as teens, meaning they could put nearly everything from their paycheck toward the first property. Second, they had a plan from the start and stuck with it. Finally, they stayed disciplined in their work. They didn't have to quit school, but they did have to carefully pick and choose how they spent their time off from work. But they got it done! And as their story emphasizes, the hardest investment is the first one. Ideally, the first investment gets the ball rolling, letting you use the momentum from it for your second, third, and every other investment after. Less than 90 days after their first house purchase, they purchased a second rental property . . . dream big, have a plan, work hard and you will see your wildest dreams come true!

In addition, REITs make for an excellent way to get a foothold in real estate without cleaning dirty toilets or accidentally tearing down a load-bearing wall. American Tower Corp., Ventas, and Public Storage are several excellent REITs on the market currently.[9]

ENTREPRENEURSHIP AND BUSINESS

So far, this chapter has revolved around investing in things that already exist. A stock belongs to a company. Property is property. Even raw land *exists*.

But maybe you excelled in art class, love Legos, and wish to create something from the ground up. In that case, you might just be an entrepreneur.

At its most basic, an entrepreneur is someone who starts a new business.[10] They range from the founders of the mom and pop bakery in town all the way up to titans of industry like Steve Jobs, Daymond John, and even Beyoncé.

It's often exciting to be an entrepreneur. You get to build something you're passionate about. It's your baby. You control what it looks like. In addition, you get to reap the rewards of your business taking the world by storm, be it profits, fame, or otherwise.

But what does it mean to start your own business? What are your responsibilities? According to one school of thought, entrepreneurship revolves around three key ideas, developed by economists Joseph Schumpeter, Frank Knight, and Israel Kirzner:

> *Schumpeter suggested that entrepreneurs—not just companies— were responsible for the creation of new things in the search for profit. Knight focused on entrepreneurs as the bearers of uncertainty and believed they were responsible for risk premiums in financial markets. Kirzner thought of entrepreneurship as a process that led to the discovery of opportunities.*[11]

Yikes! Entrepreneurship sounds a bit scary. And it is. More importantly, it's not for everyone. It's not enough to have a ground-breaking idea. You have to be able to sell it to investors so that you have the money to make it happen. You have to constantly navigate your company through hardship, which comes in various forms. If you own the mom and pop bakery, how do you respond when a competitor bakery opens across the street? If you're Google, how do you respond when the US government sues you over an illegal monopoly? [12]

And perhaps most crucially, as the head of a business, you accept the risk associated with it, including any liability for it failing.

As a teen, that pressure is nauseating. After all, you're just trying to make it through the day without anyone calling you out for wearing the same shirt twice in one week. But more than the pressure, most teens say that they have an idea for a business, but are dissuaded by not knowing where to start.[13]

To give you a bit of a head start, here are five steps aspiring entrepreneurs can take as teens to get things started.

1. **Identify everyday problems and do market research.** Being an entrepreneur is about seeing a problem in the marketplace and fixing it. For instance, maybe your city doesn't provide a leaf-collection service in the fall. It can be annoying for homeowners

to do all that raking, only to see the leaves pile up at the edge of a driveway.

As an entrepreneur, you could start a business that collects those leaves and discards them for a fee. Boom! Problem solved!

By finding a problem that needs solving, you're also ensuring that there will be demand for your goods or service. And a lack of interest or demand is a critical reason behind the failure of many young businesses.

2. **Network and follow successful entrepreneurs.** This is similar to the "Get a Real Estate Mentor" tip mentioned earlier in this chapter. Find entrepreneurs on social media and follow them. Chances are, they'll post tips and tricks of the trade, which is information you can use to kickstart your own future.

   While networking may not sound like the *most* fun activity in the world, communication is a critical tool you'll need to learn if you want to successfully grow your business.

3. **Organize your finances.** Shocker—starting your own business is going to require money (also known as capital). Go ahead and get your finances organized, make a savings plan, and get started putting aside money to fund your future business.

4. **Read books on entrepreneurship.** There are hundreds of entrepreneur-based books out there, just waiting to be thumbed through. And getting your hands on them (or an audiobook/podcast) could be the difference between being a decent entrepreneur and Warren Buffett, who credits reading 500 pages per day as his secret to success.[14]

5. **Enroll in an entrepreneurship program for teens.** If you can't get enough of the classroom, there are plenty of entrepreneurship

programs out there that cater to teens. These programs vary in function (and cost), with some serving as a how-to guide and others as actual pitch meetings with potential investors.[15]

Before bringing this chapter to a close, check out this snippet from entrepreneur and Dallas Mavericks owner Mark Cuban, who said that the worst career advice he ever got was *follow your passion*:

"No. Follow your *effort*. No one quits anything they're good at. If I followed my passion, I'd still be trying to play professional basketball."[16]

THE REAL WORLD . . . In this chapter's Real World segment, we're going to highlight some actual teenage entrepreneurs and how they managed to grow their business from idea to investment.[17] Pay especially close attention to where the inspiration for these business ideas came from (spoiler alert: most didn't have to look much further than home).

Moziah Bridges, *Mo's Bows*—Moziah Bridges started his company by taking a skill—his ability to tie a bow tie, learned from his grandmother—and a need in the marketplace—a lack of bow ties for children. After some advice from mom, he created an Etsy page and established his own business selling self-styled bow ties to youngsters.

Rachel Zietz, *Gladiator Lacrosse*—At 13, Rachel Zietz attended an entrepreneurship workshop where she was instructed to develop a business model around a need in her own life (there's that word again!). A strong lacrosse player, Rachel oriented her business plan around developing gear that wouldn't wear out so easy from the extremely physical sport. After locating a warehouse to assemble the gear and working with her parents to take out a business loan, she filled that original need by selling high-quality lacrosse gear at a reduced price. Two years later, her company was valued at over $1 million.

Shubham Bannerjee, Braigo Labs—Another teen who saw a clear need in the market, Shubham Bannerjee took something he loved—Legos—and developed a Braille printer for entry in his school's Science Fair. But Shubham's creation didn't just fit a tangible need—a Braille printer—but an intangible one as well—his printer sold for a fraction of what many on the market went for. After giving the design away for free, he secured investing from Intel to develop an improved model. In other words, he might have to leave the Legos at home.

SUMMARY

Investing comes in many different shapes and sizes. While you may not be ready to pay for a residential property in cash or swap options on the stock market floor, you can take small steps to prepare yourself for that future as a teenager. As you build those healthy investment habits, make sure you're mindful of these five common teenage investing pitfalls:

1. Burning Out

Many of the pitfalls on this list result in simply quitting before you give the practice a fair shake, and burnout is a classic pitfall when it comes to investing. It's easy to get initially excited about an investment opportunity or even the concept itself. You make a list of stocks and watch them every day for a few weeks. But soon, you lose interest. Maybe the basketball season starts back up or you have to focus on your role in the upcoming school show. Whatever the case, your inability to keep that passion alive is called burnout, and it typically comes when you can't sustain a certain level of activity.

Start small (like 15 minutes a day) and feel the rush of excitement when you succeed. By doing so, you'll develop good habits on the micro scale that will pay off in a big way down the road.

2. Not Diversifying Portfolio

When you make investments, you want to ensure that your portfolio is diverse. It's the financial equivalent of not putting all of your eggs in a single basket. For instance, what happens if you only invest in oil-related companies and there's an oil spill? Or only invest in stocks and the market experiences a recession? Or only invest in real estate and the housing market collapses, like it did in 2008?

A diverse portfolio ensures that you're covered, even if one investment falters.

3. Starting Late

Think about those teen entrepreneurs highlighted above. Thanks to starting when they did, they now have the freedom to make their own financial decisions. Moreover, their successful businesses will look excellent on any job, college, or loan application in the future. Additionally, they struck while the iron was hot. You never know if someone is working on the same golden idea as you, so the sooner you get it out there, the greater command of the market you'll have.

4. Getting Discouraged

There's no way around it: you need to have thick skin when it comes to investing. In all likelihood, your first idea won't generate a million dollars. But there might be important lessons learned along the way that will help you on your journey towards a strong financial future. Just because something doesn't work out the first time doesn't mean you don't have a future, it just means that *this particular* idea didn't work.

5. Not Doing Enough Research

Each of those teenage entrepreneurs mentioned earlier conducted at least some research before launching their business. As a result, they were able to identify a clear need in a given area and fill it. While your idea for a social media service where people can message and share videos might sound great, it's already taken (see: Instagram). You need to conduct serious research before starting a business or making an investment to determine your likelihood of success (and whether the idea has already been taken!).

Here are a few exercises to get you started on your investment grind:

Develop a Few Small Business Ideas
Entrepreneurship isn't just about starting the next mega-business. Start small—take something you're good at and find a way to turn it into a job. Here are a few ideas:

- If you like photography . . . offer your services as a birthday/event photographer

- If you're a strong student . . . offer your services as a peer tutor

- If you like playing video games . . . look into setting up a YouTube channel or blog about your favorite game

- If you like animals . . . offer your services as a petsitter or dogwalker

Make a List of Stocks/Potential Investments
Consider this part of the research phase. See what the experts are saying about the best investments right now and make a list of the few that continue cropping up. List them out, follow their prices for a month, narrow down the list and then make a pitch to your parents to open up a Youth Investment account through a service like Fidelity or Charles Schwab.

BEGIN BY . . . Determining your risk tolerance. If you need to go back to Chapter 6, that's fine! But figure out how much risk you're willing to take on in your first few investments and select a crop of stocks accordingly.

EXERCISE

Make a Savings Plan

If starting a business or financing an investment in real estate is your dream, you'll need serious dough to get started. To that end, you'll need a savings plan that maps out your income and how long it'll take to have enough money to start investing. Follow this financial plan diligently to achieve your goals!

BEGIN BY . . . Setting up a meeting with a financial advisor. Maybe your parents have their own advisor currently; there's nothing wrong with asking if they'll schedule a meeting for you, as well. This advisor can help you make a savings plan so you'll be investing in no time!

ENDNOTES

1. Buffett, W. (2002, July 18), interview: University of Georgia's Institute for Leadership Advancement, https://www.youtube.com/watch?v=2a9Lx9J8uSs.

2. Adams, R. (2023, August 18), 12 Stocks for Kids: Kid-Friendly Stocks to Begin Investing [2023], Young and Invested, https://youngandtheinvested.com/stocks-for-kids/.

3. Roberts, C. (2021, February 17), Eight Reasons You Should Consider Real Estate Investing, Forbes, https://www.forbes.com/sites/forbesrealestatecouncil/2021/02/17/eight-reasons-you-should-consider-real-estate-investing/?sh=588677365c51. Reprinted with permission.

4. Richardson, S. (2023, July 13).Types Of Real Estate Investments: Everything You Need To Know, Rocket Mortgage, https://www.rocketmortgage.com/learn/types-of-real-estate-investment.

5. Voight, K. (2023, September 6), Best-Performing REITS: How to Invest in Real Estate Investment Trusts, NerdWallet, https://www.nerdwallet.com/article/investing/reit-investing.

6. Folger, J. (2023, May 18), Best Real Estate Crowdfunding Sites, Investopedia, https://www.investopedia.com/best-real-estate-crowdfunding-sites-5070790.

7. Under 30 Wealth, (n.d.), How Can Teenagers Get Started Investing In Real Estate?, https://under30wealth.com/how-can-teenagers-invest-real-estate/.

8. Hostfully, (n.d.), Airbnb Age Requirement: Everything You Need to Know, https://www.hostfully.com/blog/airbnb-age-requirement/#:~:text=s%20age%20requirements.-,How%20old%20do%20you%20have%20to%20be%20to%20rent%20an,18%2C%20just%20the%20account%20owner.

9. Duggan, W. (2023, September 12),9 of the Best REITs to Buy for 2023, US News and World Report, https://money.usnews.com/investing/slideshows/best-reits-to-buy.

10. Hayes, A. (2023, May 09), Entrepreneur: What It Means to Be One and How to Get Started, Investopedia, https://www.investopedia.com/terms/e/entrepreneur.asp. Reprinted with permission.

11. Ibid.

12. Kerr, D. (2023, September 12), United States takes on Google in biggest tech monopoly trial of 21st century, NPR, https://www.npr.org/2023/09/12/1198558372/doj-google-monopoly-antitrust-trial-search-engine.

13. LogoLife (2022, October 06), How To Get Started As a Teen Entrepreneur, https://logolife.org/how-to-get-started-as-a-teen-entrepreneur/.

14. Natfluence, (2023, February 08), Why Reading Business Books May Actually Help You Get More Money, https://natfluence.com/how-to-get-more-money-reading-business-books/.

15. TeenLife, (2022, May 13), Are You a Young Entrepreneur? These Organizations Can Help!, https://www.teenlife.com/blog/young-entrepreneur/.

16. Rampton, J. (2023, March 16), Mark Cuban Says "Follow Your Passion" Is the Worst Career Advice You Can Get. Here's Why., Entrepreneur, https://www.entrepreneur.com/living/mark-cuban-says-follow-your-passion-is-the-worst-career/447293.

17. Oxford Royale, (n.d.), 14 Teen Entrepreneurs and How They Succeeded, https://www.oxford-royale.com/articles/14-teen-entrepreneurs/.

Chapter 8

THE TAX TALK

The hardest thing in the world to understand is the income tax.
　—Albert Einstein

Money is numbers, and numbers never end. If it takes money to be happy, your search for happiness will never end.
　—Bob Marley

Watch your parents (and any adult in your life) closely this April. See how their demeanor changes—the smiles are fewer and further between, the wrinkles lining their foreheads get a little deeper, and family movie night is likely to be dominated by total downers.

And while you may not be entitled to a cash settlement if a loved one experiences these symptoms, just know they'll pass. Because April showers bring May flowers. And although April taxes, May relaxes.

In this chapter, you'll learn all about taxes—why they exist, why we pay them, where they go, and how they work.

TAXATION WITHOUT REPRESENTATION

We're conditioned to hate taxes. We feel the same way about taxes as we do broccoli. Or snakes. Or math.

Think about it—Americans are taught to hate taxes from birth. Our story literally begins with a bunch of pissed-off colonists dumping tons of tea into Boston Harbor to protest . . . wait for it . . . taxation! So is it any surprise that some 250 years later, Americans' relationship with taxes is like a Taylor Swift fan's relationship with John Mayer?

And while you can choose to never listen to *Slow Dancing in a Burning Room* again, you cannot run from taxes. They're unavoidable, like that zit between your eyebrows that just won't go away. And while it's easier to just hate them, it's important that you know what exactly it is your taxes are funding. Because the more you get to know taxes, the more you might come to appreciate the reason we have them.

Unlike John Mayer, of course.

What are taxes?

Great question. Let's start with square one—"Taxes are mandatory contributions levied on individuals or corporations by a government entity—whether local, regional, or national."[1] In other words, taxes are the money we pay to the government so that the government has enough money to function.

Why do we have taxes?

Let's say you're one of those super granola people who shop exclusively at Patagonia and drive (or plan to drive) a Subaru Outback. You're going to fill up the bumper of that Outback with National Parks stickers, right?

Ask yourself, *how do those parks run?* There are park rangers to pay, shelters to build, and trails to maintain. And, unsurprisingly, these things cost money.

So how does the government make the money to pay for the park's upkeep? It doesn't really sell anything like a traditional business. Sure, it collects a fee when you pay for a park pass, but that hardly covers everything.

In order to keep the park's lights on, the government collects taxes. And the taxes go for way more than just the National Parks—they pay for things like Social Security, the construction of schools and roads, and waste management. Almost anything provided by the government (including local, state, and federal) is paid for through your tax dollars.

The tax rate, or the amount you're required to pay, is set by the government. On the federal level, the Internal Revenue Service and the Department of the Treasury are responsible for tax collection.

What are the different types of taxes?

So, here's the drawback: there are *a lot* of taxes. While the function might vary, the form is essentially the same: the government is taking money from a given bottom line.

Here are a few common examples of taxes in the United States:

- Income tax—money taken out of an individual's income and given to the state or federal government[2]
- Payroll tax—money withheld from an employee's pay by an employer, who in turn pays it to the government on the employee's behalf to fund Medicare and Social Security programs[3]
- Corporate tax—a slice of corporate profits taken as tax by the government to fund federal programs[4]
- Sales tax—taxes on goods/services you buy from the store or online, generally[5]
- Property tax—a tax on the value of land and property assets[6]
- Tariff— taxes on goods the government imports, which is designed to strengthen domestic businesses[7]
- Estate tax—you might have heard this called the "death tax," it's the amount applied to the fair market value of property in a person's estate at the time of death[8]

You'll notice that not all of these taxes are collected from individual people. Some, like the corporate tax, take a certain percentage out of a company's earnings, which is one of the few, few benefits of treating a company like a person.

In addition, the way these taxes are levied varies. Sales tax, for instance, is taken the moment you tap your credit card at the checkout counter. But income tax, on the other hand, is taken out whenever you receive a paycheck (or, if you are self-employed, it might only be taken on a quarterly or yearly basis).

Outgoing income

Let's hone in on income tax for a moment. As a teen, this is probably the likeliest tax you'll encounter first. Let's say you work a job at $15 an hour and work 25 hours over two weeks. In theory, this comes out to $375 in income, right?

But when you examine your pay stub, you might be surprised to see a bit less than $375. That's because the government has withheld the income tax owed to both the state and federal government (unless you're one of the lucky few who live in one of the 9 states without any income tax).

The United States operates on a progressive income tax structure, meaning you pay more in taxes based on the amount of money you make. The different tax rates are known as "brackets," and as a teen, you'll probably fall into one of the lower tax brackets. As of 2022-23, the US has seven different tax brackets, beginning at 10% and capping out at 37% for the highest earners.[9]

The amount of money your employer sets aside in taxes is determined by a number of factors. But keep in mind, when you work an hourly job, it's impossible to know exactly how much you'll make in a year. As a result, an employer might place you in a higher tax bracket, meaning more money is taken out of your paycheck on a monthly basis.

But have no fear! To get around this over-taxation problem, we have a handy thing called a "tax refund." In April, you'll fill out your taxes, where the total amount you earned in a year will be tallied up. If you made less than $11,000, you'll be in that first tax bracket (10%). But what if your employer has taken out 12% in taxes all year (which puts you in the second bracket)?

At this point, you'll be reimbursed for any additional taxes taken out during the year. In other words, that 2% (the difference between 12% and 10%) will be sent back to your account!

It's not uncommon for teens to experience the rush of a tax refund in April. It's exciting to get a few bucks back a few weeks before summer vacation.

But it's likely not something that's going to last. As you get older, chances are you'll be paid on salary, meaning you'll know how much you make in a year, giving your employer an accurate ability to calculate your tax bracket. In some cases, you might even *owe* money if your employer underestimated your tax bracket. And that's why April is often a no-good, very bad time of year for adults.

THE REAL WORLD... Here's an excerpt of a story from one parent who has some ideas about getting teens involved in tax season.[10] Parts of the original have been cut for clarity and concision.

I have to admit that April has me feeling kind of antsy this year. Add a pair of teenage wage earners to the mix, and we're feeling flummoxed by the looming financial bull's-eye that is mid-April.

While I'm not as diehard as my own dad — who way back in the '80s insisted I declare my babysitting money via paper forms (which I filled out by hand with a No. 2 pencil at the dining-room table during March break) — I found it impossible to ignore the trio of W-2s that arrived in January for my 18-year-old college student.

Like most parents in my shoes, I could really use a teen tax primer — so I reached out to an expert with an open-ended question: When should my teen start filing taxes?

"If the young person's 2022 earned income or W-2 wages is $12,950 or less, they don't even need to file an income-tax return — they're exempt," said Karla Dennis, the founder and CEO of Karla Dennis & Associates.

If that same young person has unearned income in excess of $1,150 — defined by Dennis as "money they made but didn't have to physically work for," such as proceeds from the sale of crypto-currency, for instance — they are going to need to file a tax return. Ditto for any cash earned via side hustles and odd jobs in excess of $400 that's not reported on a W-2.

Dennis, herself a parent of four, views the conversations as ed-ucational. "It's a great lesson, their first financial lesson — how to be compliant with the revenue department," she said — and that includes something as simple as babysitting money that in this day and age is easy to track.

"We live in an electronic world now," said Dennis, pointing to a proliferation of bill payments, Venmo transactions, and electronic

money transfers — all of which are tracked by the IRS. In other words, if there was ever a time for full financial transparency, that moment has arrived.

Dennis underscores the importance of engaging young people in meaningful conversations about the importance of paying taxes and, more specifically, instances where tax dollars are at work in their communities. Amenities from libraries and public parks to schools and emergency-response teams are funded by tax revenue. As such, Dennis suggests empowering teens to tackle their income taxes independently.

"Young people are so tech savvy, they should definitely file their income taxes themselves," said Dennis, who suggests pointing teens toward free online-filing services, like those available through irs.gov.

Being mindful of deadlines (from when tax documents should be available to the cutoff for filing without penalty) is another important piece of the puzzle in an increasingly online world where W-2s may not be mailed, for instance.

"Filing for an extension with the IRS is an extension of time to file, not an extension of time to pay," said Dennis of an often misunderstood scenario among taxpayers regardless of their age.

In the end, young people are like sponges. If they witness adults agonizing over paying taxes and complaining about the unpleasant process, they will likely follow suit. In this way, filing income taxes is not unlike going to the dentist.

"Young people need to understand that when you earn money, you have obligations, and the first is to pay your income tax," says Dennis. And parents can help make the tax process pain-free for their progeny — a gift that keeps on giving.

SUMMARY

Taxes are as ever-present as they are confusing. Just take the real world example from above—even adults struggle with all of the ins and outs.

While teens may not have to jump through quite as many hoops as adults when it comes to paying taxes, it's still important to develop a foundation for understanding how taxes work. Sure, it's less money in the bank, but those tax dollars are going to pay for necessary public works like hospitals, parks, and schools.

Here are a few common mistakes teens make when it comes to taxes:

1. Not Filing

File this one under "illegal" instead of "mistake." If you make any money in the year, you're required by law to file a tax return. Failing to file a tax return is punishable by a fine or even time in custody. And before you start—"not knowing" you had to file a tax return isn't an excuse under the law. And know that you've read this chapter, it's even *less* of an excuse.

2. Not Understanding

Taxes are no doubt confusing. And failing to understand taxes can lead to problems down the road, including incorrectly filing taxes. This is why it's on you to make sure that you completely understand the ins and outs involved in taxation. Don't be afraid to reach out with any questions—the parent in our real world example did just that and is probably extremely grateful. Again, noncompliance isn't really an option, so it's best to start developing a basic understanding that will help you down the line.

3. Clutter and Disorganization

As a teen, you might have income from several different places. But come tax time, you'll need to have any and all payroll documentation ready to fill out your taxes correctly. As a result, it's even more important to stay organized with your pay stubs and any other payroll documentation from an employer. Otherwise, you might find yourself digging through the dumpster to find all of your info, which is never a good place to be.

4. Having Parents Do It For You

Remember, this entire book is about teens developing good personal finance habits. It might be easier having your parents file your taxes for you, but what do you learn in the process? Absolutely nothing! It's perfectly okay to have your parents help and double-check your work. And it's okay if everything isn't perfect when you show your parents for review; the only way to learn is by making mistakes and correcting them. The point is, you're still doing the work yourself.

5. Not Appreciating

How easy is it to just hate taxes without thinking twice? Everyone does it, so who can blame you? But appreciating what your tax dollars are going toward helps take the sting out of the entire process. If you've ever had a relative need medical care at a public hospital, you helped pay for it. If you've ever taken your dog to the park, you've helped pay for it. The school you go to every day? Maybe not so cool—but you paid for it, too! Just like with investing, taxes are about putting your money to work. The only difference is that the benefit isn't just felt by you, but your entire community.

EXERCISE

Save Forms

Since being disorganized is one of the common pitfalls associated with teens and taxes, get ahead of this problem by practicing organizational skills. You'll be glad you did— organization is beneficial in just about any line of work or hobby and not limited to finance.

BEGIN BY . . . Purchasing a fireproof box to keep important documents safe. You might want to put your Social Security card, birth certificate, and any other important documents in it, including any tax/payroll documentation.

Calculate Income So Far

To get an idea of how much you've paid in taxes so far (or how much you may owe come April), calculate the income you've earned so far. You can calculate your tax figure by researching the federal tax rate (which, remember, is based on gross income) as well as your individual state's tax rate (which varies, you guessed it, by state).

BEGIN BY . . . Determine whether your taxes have already been taken out of your paycheck or whether they'll be taken out in April.

ENDNOTES

1. Gorton, D. (2023, March 31), Taxes Definition: Types, Who Pays, and Why, Investopedia, https://www.investopedia.com/terms/t/taxes.asp.

2. Kagan, J, (February 27, 2023), What Is Income Tax and How Are Different Types Calculated?, Investopedia, https://www.investopedia.com/terms/i/incometax.asp.

3. https://www.investopedia.com/terms/p/payrolltax.asp

4. Kagan, J. (2022, June 15), Corporate Tax: Definition, Deductions, How It Works, Investopedia, https://www.investopedia.com/terms/c/corporatetax.asp.

5. Kagan, J. (2023, May 30), What Is Sales Tax? Definition, Examples, and How It's Calculated, Investopedia, https://www.investopedia.com/terms/s/salestax.asp.

6. Kagan J. (2022, April 13), Property Tax: Definition, What It's Used For, How It's Calculated, Investopedia, https://www.investopedia.com/terms/p/propertytax.asp.

7. Nevil, S. (2023, May 28), What Is a Tariff and Why Are They Important?, Investopedia, https://www.investopedia.com/terms/t/tariff.asp.

8. Kagan, J. (2023, January 18), Estate Tax: Rates, Exclusions, and Impact on Gift and Inheritance Taxes, Investopedia, https://www.investopedia.com/terms/e/estatetax.asp.

9. Parys, S. & Orem, T. (2023, August 02), 2022-2023 Tax Brackets and Federal Income Tax Rates, NerdWallet, https://www.nerdwallet.com/article/taxes/federal-income-tax-brackets.

10. Van Sickle, H. (2023, April 10), I'm the mom of teens who've earned money working. This is what I learned about taxes and teens., Insider, https://www.insider.com. Reprinted with permission.

Chapter 9

SEND SCAMMERS TO THE JUNK FOLDER

Who is going to believe a con artist? Everyone, if she is good.
—Andy Griffith

Happiness comes from spiritual wealth, not material wealth... Happiness comes from giving, not getting. If we try hard to bring happiness to others, we cannot stop it from coming to us also. To get joy, we must give it, and to keep joy, we must scatter it.
—John Templeton

There are days you probably wish someone would steal your identity. Like when your parents remind you to wear sunscreen in front of the cool kids. Or when your parents remind you to wear a jacket in front of the cool kids. Or when your parents ask if you've taken your diarrhea meds in front of the coo . . . well, anyone, actually.

These moments make you feel mortified.

We replay them over and over again in our minds until we've convinced ourselves that whatever *actually* happened is way worse than what really happened. Even still, you probably want to disappear. Run away. Start a new life. Goodbye, friends and family, and hello, life on the road.

But no matter how mortally embarrassed you may feel at whatever it is your parents inevitably do, identity theft is worse. In this chapter, we're going to talk about the dishonest way of making money: scams.

You'll learn several common forms of scams, how to prevent them, and how to fight back when they happen.

Let's dive in!

TECHY TEENS

Many teens grow up with a smartphone and laptop glued to their person like an extra appendage. This has many positives: teens tend to be the most technology-savvy age group out there and are able to remain connected to friends and family.

Unfortunately, tech comes with some very serious downsides. The flip side of being connected to everyone? Anyone can seemingly reach out with an offer that is way too good to be true. And even though teens are taught never to take candy from strangers, rarely are they told not to open up emails from strangers, especially ones that look like they're from reputable sources.

Unfortunately, internet scams happen. According to the FBI, they accounted for losses amounting to $101.4 million in 2021 among teens alone.[1]

Experts have identified two critical reasons that teens tend to be targeted for internet scams.

First, teens "take longer to find out that they are victims of identity theft, thereby allowing the identity thieves more time to use their identities for criminal purposes."[2] Chalk it up to a lack of experience, slow-moving to check personal accounts, or what have you. The longer a scammer has to get away with a crime, the better the odds are that they'll get away with it.

Second, teens' "information is often used in synthetic identity theft where criminals create a phony identity with information taken from several different people."[3] Teens don't have the same financial background as an adult. This means that scammers can take the component parts of a teen's identity (Social Security Number, date of birth, etc.) and create various "fake identities" out of them. The less of a financial trail for investigators to follow, the harder it is to get to the bottom of a scam.

COMMON SCAMS

Generally, scams fall into three different categories: scams for money, scams for information, or scams for both. Let's break down a few different common examples from each category:

Scams for money

At first glance, it might seem a bit counterintuitive that teens are often the targets of money-based scams. After all, it's not like the bi-weekly paycheck from Chick-fil-A is a *massive* haul.

But what if that paycheck was multiplied hundreds or even *thousands* of times? Suddenly the scam is extremely lucrative, right? And look, teens are simply more susceptible to these sorts of scams. That's not meant to offend; it's just a fact.

Here are a few scams often targeted at teens that involve money:

- **Skill or Talent Contests**
  Beware of contests urging teens to submit a piece of artwork, musical composition, or creative essay to be judged by an "esteemed panel of experts." Usually, there will be a slew of fees associated with the contests, which are also often promised to be reimbursed should your totally Postmodern take on the Mona Lisa win. As you might imagine, no one ever wins. And the money you paid for those fees? Long gone.

- **Online Auctions**
  This one works in two different ways. On one hand, a teen wins an auction for an item that, unfortunately, doesn't exist and never comes in the mail.

On the other hand, a teen might be encouraged by an auction rep (aka, the scammer) to put an item they own up for auction, like that super-rare baseball card they got as a present for their birthday. Often, the teen will send the item in before receiving any payment, and when they reach back out to the auction rep, they've vanished.

The last one may not exactly sound like a money-based scam. But think about the ultimate purpose of the scam: to sell whatever good the scammer acquired. In that case, the teen is just one piece of the larger puzzle; preventing this type of thing from happening, though, is a great way to cut the scam off at its head.

- **Cellphone Freebies**
This one might be a bit dated, but it's still out there. Scammers will sometimes offer free ringtones or wallpapers; all the teen has to do is sign up to receive them. But hidden in the fine print might be language that signs the teen up for expensive fees.

- **Weight Loss Scams**
This one's pretty despicable, as it plays on a teen's natural anxiety about the way they look. It's no secret that youngsters often feel self-conscious about their appearance; over 65% of parents say their children feel insecure about the way they look, according to one study.[4]

Scammers have weaponized this insecurity and used it to advance their own nefarious purposes. That includes advertising for free-trial weight-loss drugs that eventually turn into an expensive, long-term contract and doctoring images to seal the deal.

Scams for information

Money isn't the only thing scammers are after. In a world where everything is connected digitally, information is the most dangerous weapon a scammer, company, or person can access.

Ever see an ad on social media that you feel was *specifically* targeted for you? You buy one cute and comfy graphic tee online, and suddenly your feed is swamped with ads for comfier and cuter graphic tees. That's not an accident. Companies share this data all the time to deliver content they think you want and, in turn, get you to spend money.

Now, what if someone had all of your personal information and could use it to make all kinds of terrible decisions *in your name*? The ramifications are horrific! Think back to our chapter on opening a bank account. We discussed the requirement of having your personal information handy, right? What if a scammer had that same information? They could open up various bank accounts in your name! They could get a high-interest credit card and push it to its spending limit! They could take out loans, and mortgages, and apply for student aid—all under your name.

Scammers are the ones making the purchases, but because they're using your information and name, it's going to affect your credit score. Which we all know is a very, very big deal.

This type of scam is called identity theft because, well, the information stolen is how companies and the government know that you're you. Sure, a scammer might not need to know *every personal detail* about your identity (like how your favorite color is aqua and you still sleep with a night light), but those details aren't really relevant to your financial identity.

While companies have developed more ways to keep our personal information safe (think name, date of birth, Social Security number, mother's maiden name, etc.), the fact that information is so valuable makes it an increasingly vital target for scammers. While money scams might net a few bucks here and there, the benefits for a scammer to completely impersonate someone else and leverage their financial identity for their own benefit are nearly limitless.

Overlap—Scams for money and information

In many cases, a scammer's goal is to collect both a teen's money and/or their personal information. Here are a few examples of scams that often overlap between the two goals:

- **Social Media Scams**

  Well, just about anything you see on this list can technically be classified as a "social media scam." Think about it—how much is social media plugged into your life? It probably has pretty immediate access to your first and last name, maybe where you live, close friends and family, even.

  For our purposes, social media scams are those that occur when someone reaches out to you via social media. Generally, these scammers will attempt to befriend you or tell you about a survey or contest designed to get you to divulge private information.

  By going the friend route, a scammer is likely to request that you send them money with a promise that they'll repay you later. Spoiler alert: No matter how deep your conversations with these online friends get, the scammers will very much *not* pay you back. And by the time you realize it, they'll have vanished in the wind.

- **Online Shopping Scams**

  As social media is often utilized by businesses to promote their goods, this one can be especially tricky. Say you're scrolling on Instagram and see a sick new lacrosse stick. It's just in time for the new season, and you could use some new gear.

  Even better? The new stick is being sold by this site for a fraction of what you'd pay in a store like Dicks. You put in all your personal information, including a credit card number, and wait excitedly for a package that, unfortunately, will never come.

If you're shopping from a site you've never heard of before, make sure you take advantage of online reviews. By searching the site's name and "reviews" or "scam" you should find plenty of information about the site's trustworthiness.

- **Camera Hacking**
  This one's especially creepy, especially given the United States' reliance on remote working and learning since the COVID-19 pandemic. The idea here is that scammers hack into the camera on a teen's laptop or phone and record them. If the teen (or anyone captured on the camera) is doing something wrong, scammers could attempt to blackmail the teen or their family. Alternatively, a scammer might try to collect information through the camera.

- **Financial Aid Scams**
  These often come in two different forms: one for scholarships or grant money and one for student loan forgiveness.[5] Generally, a scammer will send a message that a teen has won a scholarship; all they must do is pay to claim it or verify their eligibility. Either way, the scam is hoping to acquire money or a teen's personal or credit card information. Scammers may even require a teen to send over their FAFSA information, which contains just about as much sensitive financial data as any other document.

FIGHTING BACK

It's incredibly important to keep an eye out for scams, especially as a teenager. This entire book, up to this point, has been about making sound financial decisions to set you up for the future. By falling into a scam, you threaten to see your bank account drained, your progress stalled, and your financial future delayed before it even begins.

It's never your fault that you're targeted in a scam. That would be like saying it's your fault for having acne—it's simply a product of your age. But like scrubbing your face every night in the shower, there are steps you can take to prevent a scammer from gaining access to your information and your money.

If you see an email from an unknown sender that looks sketchy, send the email to the junk folder. If someone is advertising expensive tickets for significantly cheaper than they can be found at most well-known resellers, think twice before pressing "Pay Now." Just because someone seems nice in social media DMs does not mean you should tell them the name of the street you grew up on and the name of your first childhood pet.

And finally, don't be embarrassed to admit when you think you might have been scammed. At the beginning of this section, you learned that one of the biggest reasons teens are targeted in scams is because of how long it takes to uncover the scam in the first place. Don't let pride or fear get in the way of reporting a scam when you think it's occurred—it could be the difference between getting your money/information back or losing it for good.

At the end of the day, you may be a teen, but you still have common sense. It's your greatest tool to ward off scammers.

FRAUD PREVENTION

After reading all of that, it might feel like the entire universe is out to get you. But this isn't a Hans Christian Andersen fairy tale; you aren't a damsel in distress. There are several steps you can take in order to prevent fraud before it occurs.

Here are five tried and true tips from a professional financial advisor.[6] They range from super-techy options for the savviest of teens and low-tech alternatives for folks who still believe in the expediency of the fax machine:

1. **Protect your phone and your computer with a password.** This one has to be obvious, right? Most people intuitively keep their tech locked up with a passcode. But let's take it a step further because 1234 ain't cutting it these days.

   According to Financial Advisor Alan Cakebread, an excellent way to develop a strong password is by starting off with something easy and memorable.[7] Here's what he advises:

   - *Think of a phrase or sentence with at least eight words. It should be something easy for you to remember but hard for someone who knows you to guess. It could be a line from a favorite poem, story, movie, song lyric, or quotation you like. Example: "I Want To Put A Dent In The Universe"*
   - *Remove all but the first letter of each word in your phrase: IWTPADITU*
   - *Replace several of the upper-case letters with lowercase ones, at random: iWtpADitU*
   - *Now substitute a number for at least one of the letters. (Here, we've changed the capital "I" to the numeral 1): iWtpAD1tU*
   - *Finally, use special characters ($, &, +, !, @) to replace a letter or two -- preferably a letter that is repeated in the phrase. You can also add an extra character to the mix. (Here, we've replaced the "t" with "+", and added an exclamation point at the end.) : iW+pAD1tU!*

   Oof! Good luck cracking that code, scammers! In addition to this method, platforms like Apple IOS will generate random, increasingly difficult passwords when setting up new accounts. Even better—Apple and Google will store those passwords on a virtual "keychain," so you don't have to keep them all memorized.

2. **Beware when browsing unsecured wi-fi networks.** Did you know the United Nations considers access to the internet a human right?[8]

You might have already come to expect free internet wherever you go, be it a coffee shop, library, or apartment.

But these free spots are often the most vulnerable to scammers and hackers, who can use them to see any activity you've conducted through the free wi-fi. As such, avoid any banking transactions or accessing personal accounts when connected to these unsecured Wi-Fi networks, if possible. You might also consider setting up a Virtual Private Network (VPN) through a credible service, which encrypts your internet activity and keeps you safe in the process.

3. **What is in your wallet (or purse)?** No, this isn't an advertisement for Capital One. Instead, it's a reminder that you don't need your social security number to buy groceries. You don't need a bank statement to hit the movie theater. Leave those documents at home and minimize the risk if your wallet or purse gets stolen.

4. **Review financial statements regularly.** Once upon a time, you had to wait for your bank statement to come in the mail. But thanks to those handy smartphones, you can check your financial info anytime, day or night. Keeping up with them regularly will help you spot any problems or purchases you don't recognize, which is often a surefire sign of fraud.

5. **Get a shredder.** And, on the off chance that you still receive paper mail with personal information, it's best just to shred it. As desperate as it sounds, scammers and fraudsters won't hesitate to search through trash cans to find sensitive financial information. If it's all still intact, it's an easy win for the scammers; shred it, though, and you're in the clear.

THE REAL WORLD . . . Our real-world example for this chapter comes from a financial advisor and, more importantly for this section, a parent.[9] Here's how uses storytelling to prepare his teens to avoid falling into the traps laid by scammers:

This morning like every Thursday morning I took out the recycling bins for pickup. As I was preparing I noticed some loose papers that generally are not meant for residential recycling. I took a look. One of my kids had cleaned up their room and tossed out a bunch of papers.

Here is what I found:

- Full name, date of birth, address and telephone number
- Banking information (Blank cheques, credit card info with PIN)
- Health Card info
- Medical info (Condition and medications)
- Driver License info
- Cell Phone contract with full details
- Greeting Cards from family
- Employment info (Company, location and job training)

When I first realized what I found I was initially mad. Then my feelings turned to guilt. Had I taken the time to educate my young adult about how fraudsters get personal information to commit crimes? Sure they have heard of terms like Fraud, Identity theft and Dumpster diving. Do they understand what they mean?

This is particularly embarrassing because I have been working in the field of public safety and investigations for three decades. So as I educate my own children about the risks associated with personal information I thought I would share some best practices with you to share with your teens or young adults.

Here is an example: David is a "Dumpster Diver" he goes through people's trash looking for information that he can exploit for financial gain. David is either going to use the information himself or sell it. One day David comes across a recycling bin at the curb in the neighborhood that has several items that have been discarded containing personal information. This included a credit card welcome letter (including pin) and a driver's license for one of the home's residents, Kevin. David now has the following:

Kevin's full name

Kevin's full address with postal code

Kevin's date of birth

Kevin's Driver License number

Dumpster David is going to use this information to his advantage. He has enough information to call Kevin's Bank and impersonate Kevin. David may be challenged with an ID verification question, usually something as simple as "What is your Postal Code", which David has.

Dumpster David goes online and searches Kevin's social media. David finds out that Kevin has a dog named "Buster" A pet's name is a common challenge question. David also finds Kevin's mom on Facebook using both her married name and maiden name. Another common challenge question.

Armed with this information David attacks and gains full control of Kevin's bank account, David could change the mailing address on the account. David could order a new credit card delivered to the new address or even take out a loan in Kevin's name.

The potential is endless once access is established.

SUMMARY

Scams are unavoidable. You can't control being targeted by a scammer, but you can control how you respond once you know something's up. Here are a few common mistakes teens make when they encounter a scammer:

1. Opening Links from Unknown Senders

A good rule of thumb: never click or open links contained in emails from unknown senders. This isn't always the case, but the chances you actually *do* have a long lost cousin from Eastern Europe who is tangentially related to royalty and needs a few dollars to get to the throne are slim.

2. Sharing Personal Info Online

Be very careful about the information you disclose over the internet. In the case of banks, government agencies, or even most businesses, it's probably safe. For instance, you'll have to put down your credit card information to complete an online purchase at Urban Outfitters.

That said, avoid sending personal information to people who slide into your DMs or websites that you haven't vetted.

3. Failing to Speak Up

It's never too late to report a scam. But the earlier, the better. Teens are often targeted by scammers because the scammers know teens will delay reporting or discovering the scam. Even if it's a bit embarrassing, the negative effects of not reporting a scam far outweigh whatever pros there are to ignoring the problem.

4. Failing to Use Common Sense

You might have been born at night, but you weren't born last night. Teens often fall for scams because they leave common sense at the door. If any offer online seems too good to be true, your intuition should tell you that it probably *is* too good to be true.

5. Not Checking Up on Accounts Regularly

Say you check your account at the first of the month. Everything looks normal, your money is in place, no problems. If you don't check again until the last day of the month, then you've missed any potential irregularities in the account for who knows how long.

Even if you only check it every few days, that's perfectly okay. But the more often you check your account, the more likely you are to catch any problems or fraudulent purchases made on your card because of a scam.

EXERCISE

Here's the tricky part about this chapter's exercises: you can only practice what to do after being scammed *once the scamming has already started*. And we don't want to create any future Ponzi's or Madoffs.

Instead, sharpen your anti-scam IQ with some of these practice points.

Shred, Baby, Shred
Shredding non-necessary documents isn't just fun, it's borderline therapeutic. Pure catharsis.

BEGIN BY . . . keeping track of any information your bank sends via mail. While you don't necessarily want to shred everything—new cards come in the mail, after all—you can start the process by collecting any unnecessary letters and getting them ready for shredding.

Research Websites
Do some due diligence on websites that you like to shop from and search their reviews. Try websites that you know are legit—Urban Outfitters, Apple, etc.—and check up on reviews of the website. Sure, there might be a few cranky customers, but none will argue that the company is a scam.

BEGIN BY . . . The next time you come across an ad on Instagram, search reviews for the company. Chances are, if it's a scam, someone will have posted about it.

EXERCISE (continued)

Spend a Little Less Time on Socials

Oof, perhaps the hardest exercise in this entire book. While social media is great at keeping us connected to our friends, we can't escape the fact that many of the scams discussed in this chapter that target teens are conducted over social media. As a result, it might be in your best interest to spend a little less time on socials and making your digital footprint a bit smaller, and, by extension, making it harder for scammers to find an in.

BEGIN BY ... Don't quit social media altogether. Rather, see if you can spend 10 fewer minutes per day on TikTok or Instagram. Make small, easily attainable goals before trying anything too drastic.

ENDNOTES

1. Federal Bureau of Investigation, (2021), 2021 Internet Crime Report, p. 19, https://www.ic3.gov/Media/PDF/AnnualReport/2021_IC3Report.pdf.

2. Fowler, J. (2022, November 27), 10 Common Scams Targeted at Teens, Investopedia, https://www.investopedia.com/financial-edge/1012/common-scams-targeted-at-teens.aspx#citation-31.

3. Ibid.

4. Mostafavi, B. (2022, September 19), Fighting negative body image issues in kids and teens, University of Michigan, https://www.michiganmedicine.org/health-lab/fighting-negative-body-image-issues-kids-and-teens.

5. Axelton, K. (2022, August 24), 11 Common Scams Targeting Children and Teens, Experian, https://www.experian.com/blogs/ask-experian/common-scams-targeting-children-teens/.

6. Cakebread, A. (2020, May 7), Fraud Prevention for Teens and Young Adults, LinkedIn, https://www.linkedin.com/pulse/fraud-prevention-teens-young-adults-alan-cakebread/. Reprinted with permission.

7. Ibid.

8. Howell, C. & West, D., (2016, November 07), The internet as a human right, Brookings, https://www.brookings.edu/articles/the-internet-as-a-human-right/.

9. Cakebread, 2020. Reprinted with permission.

Chapter 10

COLLEGE ... IS IT FOR ME?
HOW TO SAVE AND PREPARE

The quickest way to double your money is to fold it in half and put it in your back pocket.
—Will Rogers

That person is richest whose pleasures are cheapest.
—Henry David Thoreau

Ah, college.

With one chapter left, it's only fitting that we finish up our personal finance discussion by talking about what comes next. College! But college is more than wearing your school's t-shirt or bragging about acceptance online.

Not to scare you or anything, but college is probably the biggest decision you'll make at this point in your life. College is where many people figure out what they want to do for the rest of their lives. Many people end up living in the area near where they attend. You might even find your future partner (business *or* romantic) in college!

There's a lot riding on your decision. But it's not just about *where* you go, but if you go at all. And you could pay for that decision for decades.

In this chapter, we're going to discuss the pros and cons of college, how to begin saving for school, and student loans. Along the way, think about your own future and where you see yourself. How does college figure into that plan? By the end, you should have some idea of what that future looks like.

But for now, we'll start with the basics: if college is right for you.

IS COLLEGE RIGHT FOR YOU?

Nowadays, it might feel like *everyone* goes to college. Every spring, high school seniors parade around in t-shirts announcing where they're headed in the fall. They post pictures about all of the acceptances that come in the mail (or email).

But once upon a time, college was hardly a guarantee. Around 100 years ago, only 5% of people aged 18-21 attended college. By 1950, that figure jumped to 30%.[1] By 2020, it was up to 70%.[2]

However, college admission has been on the decline lately. In 2021, for instance, only around 61% of high school seniors went straight to a four-year college or university after graduating.[3]

A combination of debt (which we'll talk about) and the desire to start earning money is usually credited for the lower rates.[4] Let's talk about the second of those factors for a moment.

Before the internet made information accessible to anyone with a decent wi-fi signal, college was *the* way to learn subjects not taught in high school. Students didn't have to learn a variety of subjects but instead could focus on one area that they wanted to dedicate their lives to. As a result, college was an excellent way to gain specialized knowledge that could then translate into a better, higher-paying job.

Today, however, things are a bit different. Entire classrooms are on the internet. Lectures can be found on free sites like YouTube. And, frankly, teens are way more savvy at technology than most college professors.

Instead of spending four years on a degree to pick up the knowledge you already have, why not begin working right away? Maybe your family owns a business that you want to join. If you grew up around the business, you probably know it like the back of your hand! Sure, you *could* spend four years getting a business degree, or you could get started making money by putting your knowledge to work.

Or maybe the job you want is best learned through an apprenticeship or vocational school. Classes in professions like plumbing, welding, car maintenance, social media marketing, photography and so much more are offered at low-cost community colleges, which will save you significant money and get you started working sooner.

Let's not kid ourselves, though. 75% of jobs out there require a college degree.[5] Even though more people are finding alternatives to the college system, a degree is still more often than not a requirement for employment. In addition, college graduates tend to earn $36,000 more per year (or 84%) than those with only a high school degree.[6]

But making money isn't the only factor high schoolers should consider when thinking about college. For the rest of the chapter, we'll talk about *spending* money. In other words—student loans.

WHAT ARE STUDENT LOANS?

If you live in one of those houses where the news is always on, you might have seen plenty of coverage of student loans recently. It's a hot-button topic that affects over 40 million Americans.

At a basic level, a student loan is any loan taken out to pay for college. College is expensive—it can cost anywhere from $17,000 to $50,000 *per year* to pay for college.[7] That's because college is more than tuition. Students have to pay for housing, textbooks, food, transportation, and a host of other expenses.

Student loans are designed to bridge the gap between what you can pay out of pocket and what you still need. Let's answer a few frequently asked questions related to student loans now.

Who can apply for the loan?

Typically, the student takes out the loan, and it goes in their name. Once it's time to start paying off the loan, it's on the student to do so.

Who gives out the loans?

For traditional loans, like a mortgage or business loan, banks hand out the cash. But when it comes to student loans, things are a bit different. Student loans are either private or public. A public student loan is given out by the Federal government via the Department of Education. These include Direct Loans, Perkins Loans, Pell Grants, and Federal Family Education Loans.

Private loans are those handed out by non-government lenders. These may include loans from companies like SoFi Technologies, Discover Financial Services, or Navient.[8]

What's the difference between subsidized and unsubsidized?

When you apply for student loans, you'll likely come across words like "subsidized" and "unsubsidized." The difference between the two is pretty significant, but for starters, a subsidized loan is for those who demonstrate financial need (based on the FAFSA form), while unsubsidized loans are open to anyone.[9]

But there are a few key differences in how the loans play out:

- Subsidized loans have their interest paid by the Department of Education until you leave school, while unsubsidized loans begin accruing interest the moment the loan is disbursed
- Subsidized loans carry a max amount of $23,000 for an entire education, while unsubsidized loans cap out at $31,000 for dependent undergraduate students and $57,500 for independent undergraduate students.
- Subsidized loans are only available for undergraduate borrowers, while unsubsidized loans are available for undergraduate and graduate borrowers.

What is the repayment plan?

In most cases, repayment begins a few months after graduation. Most loans are set for 10 or 20-year repayment plans.

What is the rate of interest?

For public loans, the interest rate is set by the Department of Education and currently is at 4.99% for undergraduate borrowers. Private loans vary, but the interest rate is generally around 12%.

Should I take out a student loan?

The answer to this question is extremely case-dependent. For starters, there could be many different reasons why one would have to take out a student loan. Maybe you can't afford to go to that one college you've always dreamed about. Or maybe you can no longer count on a sole provider to pay for your education.

The pros of student loans are fairly straightforward: college is the ticket to a better financial future (higher pay, more options, etc.), and a student loan may be the only way to get you there. A $10,000 loan may seem like peanuts when you know you can make $36,000 more per year with a college degree than without one.

But the drawbacks are there, too. At 18, you may believe you have a future in medicine that will easily pay for all your loans. But what happens when you get to college and discover your passion for the considerably less-profitable art history? You're still on the hook for those loans, no matter how big.

A big problem many folks run into when they take out student loans is that they fail to grasp what it will look like when it comes time to pay off the loan. Remember our friend from Chapter 5 who went overboard on credit card payments in college? Student loans can sometimes run into the same problems: teens take out significant amounts of money without fully understanding that they'll have to pay it all back, *plus interest.*

And, in the event you declare bankruptcy, you're still on the hook for student loans. While many of your other loans vanish (along with any semblance of a positive credit score), student loans are quite literally locked to your ankle until it's paid off.

As with just about every lesson in this book, it helps to have a plan regarding your student loans. Figure out how much money you actually *need* versus the amount you would *like* to have.

To keep your college costs down, start saving up now. Here's how to make it happen:

TIPS ON SAVING FOR COLLEGE - A TEEN'S GUIDE

It very well might cost over $100,000 to attend the college of your dreams. As a teen, that amount of money might feel unfathomable, especially when you're making minimum wage at the Foot Locker in the mall. You'd have to log *quite* a few overtime shifts to even make a dent in that figure.

That said, there's plenty you can do to keep the cost of college down. And it all starts in the classroom.

AP/IB classes or community college

Most high schools offer Advanced Placement (AP) classes, which are designed to offer high school students a college-level classroom experience. It all culminates in an AP Exam at the end of the semester. If you score high enough on those exams, colleges will let you transfer the class as college credit. Your college tuition is calculated based on the number of credits you take, so the fewer, the cheaper. And since you've already taken the AP class, it's a free credit!

The same goes for International Baccalaureate classes, although these are usually only offered at a few schools across the country.

Additionally, colleges generally use AP classes as a predictor of academic success. The more likely a student is to be successful, the more likely a school is to offer a student admission and, by extension, any financial aid. There's no magical formula for this, but it falls in line with the traditional notion that good grades help students get into college.

Similarly, a local community college might offer classes for high schoolers that can be transferred for college credit (and, in some cases, even at a discount!). Before applying, make sure that the credits do indeed transfer. Otherwise, you'll pay for classes twice—once at the community college and again at the four-year university. This option is a great way to explore different fields, like medicine or law, without significant financial risk.

Scholarships

Scholarships are free money that you can use toward the cost of college. In most cases, you must apply and, for a few high-dollar cases, interview. But scholarships are an excellent way to offset the cost of college at no cost to you. It can take quite a bit of discipline to go through with the application process, but words can't express their potential value.

While many scholarships are competitive and open to anyone, some are reserved for students who plan on studying a specific subject: medicine, politics, history, math, etc. If you're sure of what you want to study, give those a gander; the competitive pool is smaller, making it easier to stand out.

To find scholarships, use scholarship search sites like scholarships.com, FastWeb, and College Board.

Accelerated programs

Another cost-saving technique involves exploring accelerated courses of study at a college. For instance, colleges like the University of Mary offer year-round classes that let students graduate in 2.5 years instead of four.[1] While you might still pay the same rate, you'll finish quicker and enter the workforce sooner. This means more money in your pocket and sooner!

Make and save money

Whether through a job or by selling belongings you won't need in college, making money is the first step toward saving money. Any money you can put away now and save for school is money you won't have to pay off down the road in the form of a loan. For a refresher on saving, give chapter 2 another read-over.

GETTING YOUR TEENS INVOLVED IN SAVING

The college decision isn't just scary for teens. As a parent, you might feel the pressure of footing the bill when the time comes. But this process is best done when it's shared between a teen and a parent. To that end, here are a few ways to get your teen involved in the process of saving for college.

Set a savings goal

Every journey is easier when the end goal is in sight. That's true for road trips as much as it is for saving. Set a savings goal early with your teen, and be clear about the expenses you plan to pay for and what they're expected to cover. You are a team, and the team needs to have a plan!

For example, you might pay for tuition and housing, but they're responsible for paying for textbooks. Then, have your teen estimate how much money it will cost to cover the price of textbooks, and encourage them to set money aside along the way.

Stay involved

Academic success in high school is a great way for teens to lower the cost of college. But it's always easier for them when they don't feel alone. To that end, parents should stay involved in their teen's academics (but don't, you know, go overboard or anything). Attend parent-teacher conferences, ask your teen what they're learning about, and help them study for tests if they need it. Asking their teachers what talents they see in your teen is a great way to explore possible careers that you and your teen may not have considered.

The science backs this up. According to one researcher:

> *When parents become involved at school by, for example, attending events such as open houses or volunteering in the classroom, they build social networks that can provide useful information, connections to school personnel (e.g., teachers), or strategies for enhancing children's achievement. In turn, parents with heightened social capital are better equipped to support their children in succeeding in school as they are able to call on resources (e.g., asking a teacher to spend extra time helping their children) and utilize information they have gathered (e.g., knowing when and how their children should complete their homework).*[10]

If you want your teen to excel in the classroom, walk through the fire with them. Or as much as they're comfortable with.

HAVING "THAT TALK" WITH YOUR TEEN

As a teen, it can be difficult to grasp the full extent to which debt can change one's life. But as a parent, chances are you've encountered plenty of debt and/or loans. Your ability to communicate this aspect of the college process is critical.

But it can also be difficult. Especially when your teen has their heart set on an expensive option that will require a pretty significant chunk of change.

When having difficult money talks with your teen, do it in a neutral place. Go to a coffee shop, a favorite restaurant, or anywhere where your teen feels comfortable and willing to engage in a real conversation. And make sure your chat is one on one. You don't want your teen feeling outnumbered or ganged up on. In other words, it's hard enough getting a teen to listen to one adult, but two or three is nearly impossible!

Ask your teen what their thoughts are about college.[11] Here are a few questions to get the ball rolling:

- *Does she have other, less-expensive options that will provide her with the same opportunities after she graduates?*
- *What does he see as the pros/cons to the different schools he's been accepted at?*
- *What do you see as the pros/cons of each of them?*
- *What makes the specific school they have chosen "better" in his mind?*
- *Does it offer things that she won't be able to get at other schools?*
- *Do the other schools have something similar, just not quite as good?*
- *Will they earn more after graduating from the chosen school than they would at the less-expensive option? And if so, will it make up for the difference in cost? How long will it take?*
- *How much in loans would he need to take?*
- *How much will it end up costing him (including interest) to pay off the loan? How long will it take him to pay it off (keeping in mind that the longer it takes the more it will cost in interest)?*
- *Does she have a plan to pay off the loans if she has to leave school before getting a degree (loans are only deferred as long as the student is in school)?*

You might also remind your teen about the various costs associated with college, reminding them that it's more than the sticker price. Here are the various college-related expenses:

- *Required health insurance under the ACA*
- *Medical bills that insurance doesn't cover, including prescriptions*
- *Housing*
- *Food*
- *Transportation*
- *Clothing*
- *Student loan payments*
- *Entertainment, including eating out, travel, movies, concerts, etc.*
- *Emergency savings*

These conversations aren't always the easiest, but you'll feel a million times better once you've had them and get on the same page with your teen.

THE REAL WORLD . . . What if you paid $60,000 in student loans without ever making a dent in the total loan amount? Seems impossible, right? Not so for one TikTok user named Bradley, who went viral after sharing his student loan story, a reality that feels more like a nightmare.[12]

Bradley graduated college in 2013, having taken out a total of $130,000 in student loans to pay for his degree. According to him, he's never missed a loan payment and puts around $900 per month toward the loans.

As a result, he's paid roughly $60,000 on the loans. Sounds good, right? To someone without a thorough understanding of student loans, it might even sound like Bradley is close to having half of the original amount left to pay.

Guess again.

Despite paying $60,000 on the loans, Bradley owes $147,000. That's right—it's *more* than what he initially took out! This is all because of the 7% interest that he owes on the loans—nearly double the interest rate on undergraduate loans currently. As a result, his $900 doesn't even completely pay off the interest that accrues each month on the gargantuan loan.

This is why it's extremely important that you understand the parameters of a student loan before you take it out. Regardless of your job after graduating (or even if you graduate at all), you'll still be on the hook for those loans. And if you're not careful, you could find yourself nearly a decade later owing more money than you started with.

SUMMARY

As a teen, you've made plenty of major life decisions, like how to go about a prom-posal and what to wear to prom itself. But none, *none*, match the importance of college. Before cracking open a "Best Colleges" book, evaluate if college is the best option for you. Consider whether you'll need to take out student loans and how much you feel comfortable paying.

Considering the factors in this chapter will keep you from running into these five pitfalls associated with paying for college:

1. Not Researching Financial Aid Options

Plenty of teens and their families don't take the time to thoroughly research available financial aid options. This includes scholarships, grants, work-study programs, and federal student loans. Failing to explore these opportunities can result in missing out on significant financial support.

2. Ignoring Free Money

Some teens may assume they won't qualify for scholarships or grants and, therefore, don't bother applying. Or worse, classic teenage laziness and forgetfulness strikes, and the scholarship application is put off until it's too late. However, there are numerous scholarships and grants available for various talents, interests, and demographics. It's important to actively seek out and apply for as many of these opportunities as possible.

3. Relying Too Heavily on Loans

Taking on excessive student loan debt without fully understanding the long-term financial implications is a major mistake. Teens and their families would do well to

(continued) SUMMARY

consider alternative funding options before resorting to loans. If loans are necessary, they should be approached with caution, and students should have a clear plan for repayment.

4. Underestimating the True Cost of College

College is more than tuition, and many students underestimate the actual cost of attending college, including housing, textbooks, and other miscellaneous expenses. Failing to budget for these costs can lead to financial strain or the need to take on additional debt.

5. Not Considering Alternative Education Paths

While traditional four-year colleges and universities are a popular choice, they're not the only option. Community colleges, trade schools, and online programs can offer quality education at a lower cost. Teens should explore these alternatives to find the best fit for their educational and financial goals.

While college itself may still be a few ways away, there's plenty you can do to begin preparing. The following exercises are designed to get you thinking about paying for college early. That way, when the time comes, you'll be ready to make an informed decision.

Research Scholarship Options

Start familiarizing yourself with the scholarship and grant options available. The schools you apply to likely also have their own specialized scholarships that you may have to opt-into to be considered. Chances are many of the application questions and prompts are publicly available; you can get a head start on the process by thinking about how you'd complete the application, which usually includes an essay component.

BEGIN BY . . . Think about what you're interested in studying in college and research scholarships available for those specific interests. In addition, many scholarships are designed for students of underrepresented backgrounds. Cast a wide net, and feel free to narrow scholarships once you have a long list.

Play with Student Loan Calculators

It can be difficult to grasp how significant a student loan debt can be after graduating. After all, $10,000 per year might not seem like a lot. But keep in mind that $10,000 is *actually* $40,000 if you attend a four-year university. And that's *before* interest is tacked on.

A great way to forecast the complete financial cost is to calculate the gross total. Services like Bank Rate and Federal Student Aid (FSA) offer free student

(continued) EXERCISE

loan calculators. As long as you know the final amount and interest rate, you can see the complete figure. For instance, a $40,000 loan at 6% interest will accrue over $20,000 in interest and cost $337 per month to pay off in 15 years.

BEGIN BY . . . Researching the cost of tuition at a few schools. Once you have this information, you can plug them into the calculator to get an idea of how much you'll pay.

ENDNOTES

1. Mintz, S. (n.d.), Statistics: Education in America, 1860-1950, *Gilda Lehrman Institute of American History*,

2. Welding, L. (2023, August 8), College Enrollment Statistics in the U.S., *Best Colleges*, https://www.bestcolleges.com/research/college-enrollment-statistics/.

3. Ibid.

4. https://www.businessinsider.com/college-enrollment-declining-student-debt-job-market-politics-2023-3#:~:text=A%20college%20degree%20just%20might,fallen%20in%20the%20last%20decade.

5. Trend, D. (2022, August 07), 75% of New Jobs Require a Degree While Only 40% of Potential Applicants Have One, *Truthout*, https://truthout.org/articles/75-of-new-jobs-require-a-degree-while-only-40-of-potential-applicants-have-one/.

6. Association of Public & Land Grant Universities, (n.d.), How does a college degree improve graduates' employment and earnings potential?, https://www.aplu.org/our-work/4-policy-and-advocacy/publicuvalues/employment-earnings/#:~:text=Typical%20earnings%20for%20bachelor's%20degree,million%20more%20over%20their%20lifetime.

7. Song, J. (n.d.), Average Cost of College in America, *Value Penguin*, https://www.valuepenguin.com/student-loans/average-cost-of-college.

8. Ross, S. (2023, February 27), Who Actually Owns Student Loan Debt?, *Investopedia*, https://www.investopedia.com/articles/personal-finance/081216/who-actually-owns-student-loan-debt.asp.

9. Helhoski, A. (2023, June 02), Which to Borrow: Subsidized vs. Unsubsidized Student Loans, *NerdWallet*. https://www.nerdwallet.com/article/loans/student-loans/unsubsidized-student-loans.

10. University of Mary, (n.d.), "Year Round Campus," https://www.umary.edu/academics/year-round-campus. Reprinted with permission.

11. Stanford, L. (2023, July 25), Does Parent Involvement Really Help Students? Here's What the Research Says, *Edweek*. https://www.edweek.org/leadership/does-parent-involvement-really-help-students-heres-what-the-research-says/2023/07e. Reprinted with permission.

12. Kelley, M.A. (n.d.), Talking To Your Teen About College Debt, *The Homeschool Mom*, https://www.thehomeschoolmom.com/talking-to-your-teen-about-college-debt/.

13. Bjella, B. (2022, Jan. 17),'It's not his fault': Man says he paid off $60,000 of student loan debt—but still owes more than he initially borrowed, *Daily Dot*, https://www.dailydot.com/irl/student-loan-payments-interest-debt/.

CONCLUSION

W ell, we've reached the mountaintop. Now that we're here, it's easy to see how far we've come. Take a few pictures of the view; it's a great one. The cell service is admittedly spotty—construction on the personal finance mountaintop Starbucks isn't set to be finished until next month.

In all seriousness, you've come a long way.

Remember the savings chapter? How scary it felt? But we did it together and learned that maybe, just maybe, putting money aside isn't the hardest thing in the world. We took the sting out of a budget, learning how it's not meant to be something that *limits* you but a tool that *liberates* you.

How about the excitement when we got to the part about investing? After all, there's probably a bit of you who always wanted to invest, even before reading this book. Now you know how. You *even* know how to assess your own level of risk and properly diversify your investments.

Ah, and that bit about getting a job? We took the mystery out by getting you to think critically about all of the extracurriculars you're involved in and how those naturally lend themselves to some of the same traits an employer looks for in an applicant. Starting from scratch never felt so good!

And that's what we did: start from scratch. At the beginning of this book, we were at the foot of the mountain, staring at the snow-capped peak, imagining all of the things that could go wrong along the way.

While we've reached the top of *this* mountain, there's still more work to do. You have an excellent foundation, but to reach the next level (did someone say Everest?), you'll have to practice those good habits each and every day.

That may sound difficult, but never forget that you aren't alone. You may still be a beginner (even after reading this book), which is perfectly okay. Remember that everyone has, at one point or another, been a beginner at every single thing that they've done.

Literally.

That includes things you do every single day, like walking. You may not remember your first steps, but your parents probably do. And if you ask them, I bet they'll tell you that your first walk was less than perfect!

It also includes sports. You might be the leading goalscorer on your soccer team, the best blocker on a basketball team, or have the brainiest cranium on your academic team. But you had to work hard to get there.

Every day you've taken steps to become better at those activities. In other words, you've spent each day building on those first steps, honing your craft until you're talented enough to make the varsity team.

Hopefully this book does the same by offering a strong financial foundation that you can grow upon. Here's a word of parting wisdom and inspiration from a popular social media financial advisor:

Don't let the fear of being a newbie hold you back. Keep pushing, stay consistent, and who knows, you might surprise yourself along the way.[1]

The personal finance road is dark, rocky, and replete with traps. We've climbed one mountain in this book, but there are many more that you'll face as you continue along. Financial management skills are crucial as you prepare to transition into adulthood. These life-changing skills will be your foundation for financial freedom. Use the lessons in this book as your hiking gear to take the fear out of managing your personal finances!

With any luck, this book is the closest you and I will ever come to meeting each other. If you start building those good habits, avoid each chapter's pitfalls, and follow through with the exercises at the end of each section, *you'll have financial freedom for a lifetime!*

The next hike is in your hands, you've got this. Good luck.

ENDNOTES

1. The Broke Black Girl. (2023, September 09). *Gentle reminder* [Link to post attached] [Post], *Instagram*. https://www.instagram.com/p/Cw-r5M8r6gF/?igshid=MzRlODBiNWFlZA==.

www.ingramcontent.com/pod-product-compliance
Lightning Source LLC
Chambersburg PA
CBHW030515210326
41597CB00013B/921